A Bloody History of Bosque County, Texas

T. L. Harrison

DEDICATION

This work is dedicated to the families of the victims of the crimes discussed herein.

Property of The Bosque County Collection

CONTENTS

ACKNOWLEDGMENTS

This project would not have been possible without the support and assistance of many wonderful people. Firstly, I would like to acknowledge Mrs. Ruth Crawford of The Bosque Historical Commission and The Bosque County Collection Archives. Throughout this experience she has been an invaluable asset whose enthusiasm for the preservation of history is unsurpassed. I would also like to thank Researcher and Assistant Curator of Collections for the Texas Prison Museum, Elizabeth Neucere. Her tireless research allowed me rare insight into the minds of the individuals who committed these crimes. My family and friends, most notably my loving and patient husband, gave me the confidence and support to make a wild idea a reality. I cannot thank you all enough.

Please support keeping history alive:

The Bosque Historical Commission
http://www.bosquechc.org/

The Bosque County Archives
101 N Main St, Meridian, TX 76665
(254) 435-6182

Property of The Bosque County Collection

1. ARCHIBALD KELL
1855

Before ever having been established as a county, the Bosque Territory attracted far-reaching attention. The lure of land ownership and opportunity called many to the area. Still others, such as men returning from the Mexican-American war, found solace in the beauty of the land. In the winter of 1839, Captain George B. Erath led a detachment of Texas Rangers along the Bosque River to scout for signs of Indians, an ever-present threat in frontier Texas. Though the mission proved uneventful, the rangers were awestruck at the beauty of the Bosque River Valley. So much so, that they requested Erath survey the land on their behalf. It is believed that from this survey came the first locations in the Bosque Territory
1

The first permanent white settlers may have established roots somewhere around 1850. Also in 1850, approximately 125 British settlers arrived in Galveston bound for the upper portion of the Brazos River. The Universal Immigration Company of England had purchased 27,000 acres with the intention of establishing the City of Kent, which was to lay roughly three miles north of modern day Kopperl and two miles south of Kimball. Within two years, the City of Kent was abandoned. Constant threat of Indian attack and austere conditions were more than the British settlers were able to overcome. Nothing remains of the ill-fated settlement today.[2] As the City of Kent fell, other settlers arrived to populate the area. Three of those settlers, J. K. Helton, Presley Bryant, and Archibald Kell, would set into motion both Bosque County's court system and its bloody history.

Prior to 1853, the Bosque Territory fell inside the boundaries of McLennan County. It was not until late 1853 that Bosque's population grew to the point of warranting independent political representation. On February 4th, 1854, Bosque County was set apart from McLennan County. The act of legislature forming the new county's boundaries named the six men that would serve as commissioners and required that the county seat be located as close to the center of the county as possible. On June 27th, 1854, Commissioners Lowry Scrutchfield, Samuel S. Locker, Williams McCurry, Jasper N. Mabray, and William Gary met near the site of present-day Meridian. The sixth commissioner, T. E. Everett, could not attend that day for unknown reasons. It was discovered that Isreal Standerfer owned a section of land that sat precisely in the center of the county. He offered to section 100 acres of his property into town lots and sell them himself, with the county receiving 10% of the profits. It seemed like a fair arrangement until Dr. J. M. Steiner and J. P. Eubank agreed to donate land to become county seat free of charge. Even though the 120 total acres being offered by Steiner and Eubank were two miles north of the center of the county, the commissioners accepted their generous offer. Upon the suggestion of Commissioner Jasper Mabray, the seat of Bosque County was named Meridian. On August 7th, 1854, the commissioners met again. This time, their task was to carry out a vote for county offices.

Under a large oak tree that would come to be known as "Election Oak," J. K. Helton was elected justice of the peace, Archibald Kell was elected treasurer, and Presley Bryant was elected sheriff.[3]

J. K. Helton, whose full name was Joseph Knowles Helton, and his family immigrated to Texas in 1842. During their initial years in Texas, they lived in Harrison County. Helton was a farmer and rancher by trade. However, when the family moved onto a 240-acre homestead immediately west of Meridian in 1853, Helton began to take an interest in the law. In addition to his ranching duties, he became a self-educated jurist and community leader. It is likely that it was his position within the community that led to him being elected to the office of justice of the peace. In 1857, he would be admitted to the bar and in 1861, he would become Bosque County's chief justice.[4] Bosque County's first court records reflect that all manner of legal matters were addressed in Judge Helton's court. Criminal cases, family disputes, and debt mediation were all part of Judge Helton's very broad purview.

James and Elizabeth Kell, along with their five sons, Archibald, Matthew, Abraham, Francis, and Scott, moved from Rusk County to Milam County in the early 1850s. The 1850 Federal Census shows the Kell family as living in Milam and Williamson County. Archibald is listed as being 32 years old, a farmer, and having been born in Indiana.[5] The eldest brothers later moved to the Bosque territory and their parents followed. In 1854, Archibald purchased 1,256.5 acres in the area of present-day Clifton, Texas. This tract was later deeded to his brother Francis.[6] The Kell brothers bought, sold, and traded large tracts of land regularly. Property in the area surrounding the county seat, Meridian, was a valuable commodity. Due to its location in the central part of the state, some even speculated the Meridian might one day become the capital of Texas.[7]

Presley Bryant, along with this wife and children, was also

among the settlers to arrive in the Bosque Territory prior to 1853. Bryant is said to have been a Texas Ranger. However, there is no existing record of Bryant having ever served. Records retained at the Armstrong Research Center in Waco, Texas show several men with the last name Bryant serving around the time Presley Bryant is assumed to have been enlisted. Some of those men are even listed as having served under Captain Erath in the Milam County area. There, however, was no one listed with the first name Presley or a name that was phonetically similar. Historical records often contain variations in the spelling of a person's name. The spotty record keeping of the time could be to blame for this oversight. Alternately, one could also speculate that Bryant rode the coat-tails of the legendary Texas Rangers to garner respect within the community.

In 1855, Sheriff Bryant entered into a business agreement with the Kell brothers in which Bryant was loaned a substantial sum of money. A promissory note, signed on June 27th, 1855, states that Bryant would either pay back the loan prior to September 1st, 1855 or give the Kell brothers fifty bushels of corn.[8] Bryant never made good on the agreement. Handwritten court documents indicate that Matthew Kell obtained an attachment due to the unpaid debt on September 17th, 1855. The bottom of the document is signed J. N. Mabray. Mabray is believed to have been the county clerk.[9]

One of Sheriff Bryant's deputies served the attachment the same day by taking one crib of corn and fifteen hogs from Bryant's ranch. Bryant was also ordered to pay $3.80 in court costs. The document further reflects that a copy of the attachment was left with Sheriff Bryant. This would indicate that he was present when the attachment was executed.[10] It would have been an intolerably humiliating experience for a man of his standing.

Documents also reveal that later that same month, tensions between Bryant and the Kell brothers boiled over. On

September 29th, 1855, Sheriff Bryant was charged with "Shooting to Intent to Kill Archibald Kell." He was taken into custody and, with Judge Helton presiding, pled not guilty. He was released on $500 bond. When Archibald Kell succumbed to his wound on October 12th, 1855, the charge against Sheriff Bryant was amended to murder and he was arrested once more on October 15th, 1855. He, again, pled not guilty.[11] Details of the shooting are not known, partly due to the case never making it to trial. The former sheriff further disgraced himself by fleeing Bosque County and leaving behind his wife, Ruth, and their five children. He, however, did not flee far enough. The last documented sighting of Bryant was in Johnson County. He was said to have been seen leaving a gambling establishment in Buchannon, the county seat of Johnson County at the time. He was later found dead on the side of the road. A short contribution to the January 29th, 1856 edition of the *Galveston Weekly News* states:

> "A letter dated Waco, January 14th, 1856 says: "Mr. Presley Bryant, who lived in Bosque County, and has been one of your subscribers, was killed last week near Cross Timbers, by some unknown person. Bryant was the man who killed a man at Meridian, last Fall."[12]

The sheriff of Johnson County, however, believed he knew exactly who had killed Bryant. On February 22nd, 1865, an arrest warrant was issued on Abraham Kell for the offense of "Assault and Battery with Intent to Kill and Murder on the Body of Presley Bryant."[13] Abraham Kell was arrested shortly after but was bonded out. The murder of Presley Bryant, much like his own victim, never went to trial. Abraham Kell, along with his brother Scott, moved to Goliad and the case was eventually dropped. Soon after, Matthew and James Kell moved their families to Coryell County. The remaining Kell, Francis, maintained strong influence in Bosque County and established the city now known as Clifton before moving to Wichita Falls. In 1857, he and his wife had a son. They named him Archibald.

The location of Presley Bryant's grave is not known. A memorial bench has been placed in Montague Cemetery in Montague County, Texas that is dedicated to the memory of Presley Bryant, wife Ruth, and daughter Lucy. The Kell family plot is prominently featured in Clifton Cemetery in Clifton, Texas and features a large bronze statue of Francis Kell. There is a grave marked as belonging to Archibald Kell; however, dates indicate that it belongs to his nephew namesake. The first Archibald is likely buried in the plot, as well, but due to wear on some of the markers, his marker cannot be identified.

Election Oak. Photo property of The Bosque County Collection

Election Oak site marker

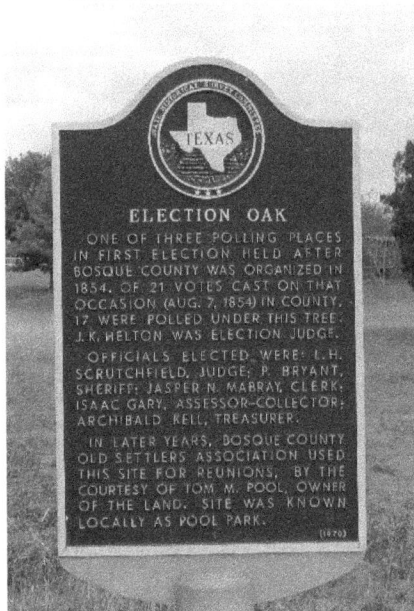

194

THE UNITED STATES OF AMERICA.

To all to whom these Presents shall come, Greeting:

WHEREAS *Archibald Kell, of Warrick County, Indiana,*

has deposited in the GENERAL LAND OFFICE of the United States, a Certificate of the REGISTER OF THE LAND OFFICE at *Vincennes,* whereby it appears that full payment has been made by the said *Archibald Kell* according to the provisions of the Act of Congress of the 24th of April, 1820, entitled "An Act making further provision for the sale of the Public Lands," for *the North East quarter of the North West quarter of Section twenty, in township four South, of Range eight west, in the District of Lands subject to sale at Vincennes, Indiana, containing forty acres,*

according to the official plat of the survey of the said Lands, returned to the General Land Office by the SURVEYOR GENERAL, which said tract has been purchased by the said *Archibald Kell*

NOW KNOW YE, That the **United States of America,** in consideration of the Premises, and in conformity with the several acts of Congress, in such case made and provided, HAVE GIVEN AND GRANTED, and by these presents DO GIVE AND GRANT, unto the said *Archibald Kell,*

and to *his* heirs, the said tract above described: TO HAVE AND TO HOLD the same, together with all the rights, privileges, immunities, and appurtenances of whatsoever nature, thereunto belonging, unto the said *Archibald Kell,* and to *his* heirs and assigns forever.

In Testimony Whereof, I, *Martin Van Buren* PRESIDENT OF THE UNITED STATES OF AMERICA, have caused these Letters to be made PATENT, and the SEAL of the GENERAL LAND OFFICE to be hereunto affixed.

GIVEN under my hand, at the CITY OF WASHINGTON, the *first* day of *February* in the Year of our Lord one thousand eight hundred and *thirty eight* and of the INDEPENDENCE OF THE UNITED STATES the Sixty *second third*

[L.S.]

BY THE PRESIDENT: *Martin Van Buren,*
By *A. Van Buren Jr.* Sec'y.
A. M. Garland, Recorder of the General Land Office.

Deed for land purchased by Archibald Kell. Courtesy of The Bosque County Collection

Attachment for debt owed by Presley Bryant. Courtesy of The Bosque County Collection

No 33

The State of Texas
vs
P. Bryant

This is an action for shooting with intent to kill. Affidavit filed and writ issued the 29th day of September A.D. 1855 and handed to John Marshall Sheriff of Bosque County — returned executed by taking the defendant Bryant into custody.

Case called the 29th day of Sept in the evening — Bryant pled Not Guilty. The affidavit of J.L. Vaughn entitled "State — Not Guilty."

Case — Continued Until — Monday the 1st day of October A.D. 1855 —

On the day of trial the Defendant was brought into Court — all parties ready for trial — The Justice of the Peace [...] testimony ordered that [...] give bond and securities for his appearance at the next Term of the District Court of McLennan County — in the sum of Five hundred Dollars —

In the above case this the 12th day of October A.D. 1855 — came Mathew Kell and filed his affidavit that Archibald Kell the person whom Bryant was bound over to Court for shooting — died this evening from the effects of his wounds —

Affidavit filed & writ issued Oct 12th 1855 — Returned Executed by taking Bryant into Custody —

Case called 15th day of October A.D. 1855 — Bryant plead — Not Guilty — After hearing the report of the Coroners Inquest and the testimony of Dr. [...] who testified that the wounds inflicted by Bryant actually killed Kell — the Justice ordered that P Bryant give Bond & security for his appearance at the next Term of the District Court of McLennan County for Two Thousand Dollars —

Warrant for the arrest of Presley Bryant. Courtesy of The Bosque County Collection

J. K. Helton. Courtesy of The Bosque County Collection

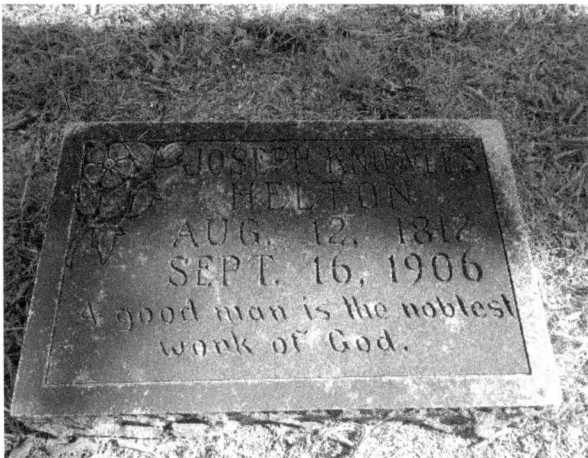

This statue of Francis Marion Kell sits at the center of the Kell family plot in Clifton cemetery. It is visible from SH 6

2. HESTER/HARVICK FEUD
1869

In the late 1850s, Ward Keeler and Ranse Walker arrived in northwestern Bosque County. Keeler was a New York native and one of Bosque County's early surveyors. He built a log cabin on his newly-settled land and welcomed a son named Ire. The cabin became the first residence in the community of Iredell, named after Keeler's son. Robert A. Hester and his wife, Rhoda Jane Medford-Hester, arrived in the area in January of 1855 from Smith County, Texas. Their third child, Mary, is said to be the first child to be born in the newly established Iredell settlement.[14] Another former Smith County resident, Nicholas "Doc" Harvick, settled the area around 1860. There is little doubt that Harvick and Hester knew each other before settling in Iredell. Smith County district court minutes show that on Wednesday, April 18th, 1849, both Hester and Harvick went to trial for criminal offenses. Hester, who had been accused of the offense of card playing, pled guilty and was fined $10.00 plus court costs. On his charge of assault and battery, Harvick also pled guilty and was fined $10.00 plus court costs. [15]

About two and a half miles east of where Iredell was to be located, Robert Hester built a log building that would house the first school in the Iredell settlement. Hester Cabin became the central community meeting place. Reverend George Washington Roberts, a Baptist minister from Alabama, also began holding services for his twelve-person congregation at the Hester Cabin in 1868. Iredell was growing and so too were the families that settled there. Establishing a thriving settlement on the Texas frontier was no easy task. From time to time, the Iredell settlement would be raided by the Indians living in the area. Although most raids resulted in loss of livestock rather than life, the settlers were nonetheless fearful. King Harvick, the eldest child of Doc Harvick, was nineteen years old in 1869. Late that year, King and some of his friends sought out some boyish fun. The young men, thinking Robert Hester a coward, decided to frighten him by pretending to be Indians and staging a raid on his home. According to a retelling of the event featured in the *Iredell Times*, Hester took the prank very seriously. Seeing the men approaching his home, he immediately secured his gun and fired at the intruders. King Harvick was killed. Once Hester realized the true identities of the men, he was overtaken with regret. To most in the community, it was an unfortunate accident. Recognizing the fault of the young man, no one blamed Hester. No one, that is, except King's father.

The Harvick family, undoubtedly, grieved the loss of their son. Throughout the rest of the winter and into spring, Doc Harvick held his grudge against Hester a secret close to his heart. On Sunday, May 2nd, 1869 Robert Hester and his six-year-old son, James Albert Hester, had just settled into their seats at the Hester Cabin for morning services. Harvick, who had followed father and son, rode up on his horse and dismounted. Instead of tying his horse, Harvick asked a young man named Koss Barry to hold the reins for him. Barry could

14

not have known of the tragedy that was about to unfold. As Harvick walked into the church, he raised his gun. He fired upon and killed both Robert Hester and his son. The congregation was, understandably, shocked and no one moved momentarily. They watched as Doc Harvick ran from the church, mounted his horse, and rode away. It was the last time Harvick would ever be seen in Iredell.[16] News sources as far away as Galveston, Texas covered the tragedy. Harvick is believed to have gone to the Indian Territory of Oklahoma where he died in 1890.

Doc Harvick's wife, Mary, remained in the area. Interestingly, many years later, a grandson of Robert Hester married a granddaughter of Doc Harvick. The Hesters are buried in the Old Williamson Cemetery, which lies about two miles east of Iredell.

Book A
Spring Term 1849

Abstract of District Court Minutes
Smith County, Texas

No. 9. Thomas G. GARDNER vs. Frost THORN and Archibald HOTCHKISS. Clerk has leave to amend endorsement of interrogations subject to exception. Case stands continued on affidavit of defendants until next term of court.

No. 10. Thomas G. GARDNER vs. Archibald HOTCHKISS. This cause stands continued on affidavit of defendant until next term of court.

No. 13. State of Texas vs. Samuel W. FARMER. Defendant moved to quash the writ. Ordered that the writ be quashed and an alias citation issue and this cause stands continued until next term of court.

No. 21. Archibald HOTCHKISS and Frost THORN vs. Thomas G. GARDNER. The parties came by their attorneys and by consent of parties this suit stands continued until next term of court.

No. 31. Woodson D. HENRY vs. James C. HILL. This day came the parties by their attorneys and by consent this cause stands continued and defendant has time to answer by or on the first day of next term.

No. 37. Frost THORN vs. Thomas G. GARDNER. Leave was given to plaintiff to amend his petition and this case stands continued as on affidavit of the plaintiff.

No. 38. William DANIEL for James M. RUSH vs. Hansford SPLAWN & William SPLA* Appeal from Justice Court. Parties by their attorneys announce themselves ready for trial. Jury: Johnathan McPETERS, Arnold O BRYAN, Richard HOLDIN, Richard LAWRANCE, Abram LOTT, John R. BUTLER, Robert HESTER, Peter MARSH, Hardy HOLMAN, Absalom L. WATTS, Francis WILLIAMS, Robert L. BRADFORD. Their verdict: Find for the plaintiffs the sum of $80.74. Plaintiff to recover of the defendants $80.74 and all legal interest, and his cost expended in this court, and the sum of $3.45, the cost in Justices Court.

No. 46. Frost THORN vs. Woodson D. HENRY. Parties came by their attorneys and this case stands continued for want of service and alias ordered.

Ordered that court adjourn until tomorrow morning at nine o'clock.

Wednesday, April 18, 1849 (the third day of the term)
No.4.
State of Texas vs. McDonald LOWRANCE. Defaulting juror obstructing execution of process. District Attorney shows the defendant has not been arrested. It is ordered that an alias capias be issued and this cause be continued.
No. 11.
State of Texas vs. Robert HESTER. Card playing. Defendant says he is guilty
Jury: Jonathan McPETERS   Arnold O'BRIAN   Richard HOLDIN
      Richard LAWRANCE   Abraham LOT   John R. BUTLER
      Peter MARSH   Hardy HOLMAN   Absalom WATTS
      Francis WILLIAMS   Robert L. BRADFORD   John LOLLAR
Their verdict: Assess a fine on the defendant of $10.00. State to recover of the defendant the sum of $10.00 and all her costs

State of Texas vs. Nicholas HARVIC. Assault and Battery. Defendant says he is guilty. Jurors are:

continued pay 21

Bosque County Collection

Abstract of District Court Minutes. Property of The Bosque County Collection

FALL TERM 1852

August 23, 1852

Following persons drawn as jurors for Fall Term of District Court:

John Farris	Robt. H. Hester	Jonathan Green	James C. Rogers
William B. Hase	Richard Beck	A. M. Dean	Christopher Farm
Walter Boyd	A. G. Atkinson	Newton Atkinson	Tarlton Bond
B. F. Mace	Jefferson Horton	Arthur Robinson	Irwin Ruckar
William Gordon	F.S. Ross	William J. Guthery	James C. Moor
Richard Lawrance	John W. Chancy	Noble Osburn	Wm. Perryman
Gabriel Jones	William N. Edwards	John L. Davis	J. M. McCain
William McMurry	Jacob Mathews	Robt. B. Hudnal	Wm. Pendergrass
D. S. Mangrum	Nicholas Harvick	C. W. Prewitt	G. W. Rector

Certified by A.J. ELLIS, Clerk D.C., Eli E. COWSAR, Clerk Co.Court, and
Green B. EPPERSON, Justice of the Peace.

October 25, 1852

Hon. Lemuel D. EVANS, presiding; S.P.DONLEY, District Attorney; John N.
McKINLEY, Sheriff by B. SCOTT, Deputy; and A.J. ELLIS, Clerk.

Not to be found in county: Jonathan GREEN, C. W. PREWITT, Irwin RUCKER.
Excused for cause were: G. JONES, Wm. McMURRY, J. MATHEWS, N. ATKINSON,
R. B. HUDNAL, J. C. ROGERS, W. J. GUTHERY.

Grand Jurors were:

J. M. McCAIN	Wm. PENDERGRASS	Richard LAWRANCE
Wm. PERRYMAN	Arthur ROBINSON	Wm. N. EDWARDS
Noble OSBURN	F. S. ROSS	Richard BECK
Walter BOYD	Tarlton BOND	D. S. MANGRUM
A. M. DEAN	Wm. B. HASE	Jeff HORTON

Under charge of N. B. LUCKEY, constable.

Remaining three jurors serve as petit jurors: R. H. HESTER, C. FARMER, and
G. W. RECTOR. Sheriff to summon nine more jurors for tomorrow morning to
serve as travis jurors.

No. 141. C. GREGORY vs. W. WILLIAMS. Attorney for defendant suggests the
death of defendant.

No. 164. EVANS,SANDERS & CO. vs. Wm. C. LEE. Plaintiffs to give security
for costs of suit.

No. 167. W. HOWETH vs. W. G. PARKER & A. CHANCELLOR. Plaintiff ordered to
give security for costs of suit.

No. 170. HAMILTON & WILEY vs. W. C. LEE. Plaintiff ordered to give security
for costs of suit.

No. 172. John JONES assignee of R. J. JONES vs. J. SENSIBOUGH. Plaintiff
ordered to give security for costs of suit.

No. 176. F. OBERTHIER vs. T. N. GREGORY. Plaintiff ordered to give security
for costs of suit.

Historical marker for First United Methodist church in Iredell

Robert Hester grave marker. Obtained from Ancestry.com

3. AMOS SMITH
1875

Despite the Hester/Harvick tragedy of 1869, Iredell pulled together as a community and continued to grow. A post office was established on December 21st, 1870 with Ward Keeler's son, William Gordon Keeler, at the helm. The first lot was sold on February 13th, 1871 to a blacksmith named William H. McLain. McLain's standing as an original resident of Iredell is reflected in the street named after him. McLain had a reputation for being fonder of liquor than most, and Ward Keeler, head of the Temperance movement in Texas, did not approve. As part of a clause in his deed, McLain was strictly forbidden from selling liquor on the premises lest his deed be revoked and his land returned to the Keeler estate. Ward Keeler passed away in 1871, when the town he created was only nine months old.

Around this time, a young man named Amos Smith (also known as Ame) arrived in Iredell. Smith, like many young men who had served in the Civil War, moved from his native Tennessee in search of new opportunities. He was about 26 or 27 years old at the time and unmarried. He was a quiet man whose unassuming and self-sufficient nature quickly earned him the respect of his neighbors.

It was not long before Ame was introduced to Samantha Ann Jones, the daughter of Mrs. Dixon Walker, one of Iredell's first settlers. She was said to be small and vivacious. On December 24th, 1867, Ame and Samantha were married by Reverend H. R. Pinell, who was one of the earliest Methodist ministers in Bosque County. Twin daughters Mary and Elizabeth came soon after on January 1st, 1869. Tragically, little Mary passed away in the latter part of 1870. When the Smiths' third daughter was born on October 9th, 1871, she too was named Mary. Shortly after little Mary's death, in an incident oddly reminiscent of the events leading to the death of King Harvick, a member of the Turnbow family decided to play a prank on Ame.

Turnbow rode through the open hallway, often called a "dog trot," of Ame's cabin while firing a pistol. Samantha and her infant daughter, Elizabeth, were alone in the house and understandably terrified. Once Ame arrived home and learned of the prank, he immediately rode to the Turnbow home where he shot and killed the man responsible for terrorizing his family. There is no record of Ame ever having been sought by the sheriff for killing the man. Iredell had not been spared the lawlessness that plagued Reconstruction Texas. Throughout much of the state, law and law enforcement had suffered a complete breakdown. Lack of confidence in the legal system frequently resulted in mobs handing down justice on their own terms. It is rumored that during the 1870s, one to two lynchings were carried out in Bosque County per week. It was not uncommon for local citizens to establish their own form of law enforcement, never involving established law enforcement entities in such matters. All things considered, it is no surprise that Ame did not face criminal charges. The event, nonetheless, established Ame's reputation as a fearless and capable husband and father.

For all of the esteem his neighbors held for him, Ame had a serious weakness. He loved to gamble. Gambling, at the time, was not only illegal but also dangerous. On one occasion, when Ame was gambling with Jim Terrell against two other men, the other men got into a disagreement. The men decided to settle the quarrel with knives. They bloodied each other and the ground considerably before Ame and Terrell decided they had best leave the two men to themselves to settle the fight. Ame's two favorite gambling companions are identified as Wood and Ledwell.[17] Rumors soon began to travel around the community that Wood and Ledwell were much more interested in Samantha than gambling with Ame. Whether an actual affair had taken place or not is an issue of great debate. What is known is that on July 26th, 1875 Ame was ambushed and shot in the back as he neared his home on horseback. Descendants of Samantha and Ame Smith believe that Ame was killed in the course of a robbery attempt. Ame had just sold property in another state and they believe that his saddlebags were filled with money on the day of the attack. The saddlebags were found empty after the murder.[18]

The citizens of Iredell at the time of the murder did not believe that robbery had anything to do with it. Suspicion fell immediately on Wood and Ledwell. Wood attempted to divert suspicion by telling Jim Terrell that he believed a local black man was responsible for the killing. Terrell did not believe Wood, and, in fact, believed him to be an accomplice in Ame's death. Terrell took Wood to a neighbor's home where he repeated the story. Neither man believed Wood and they took him into custody. Meanwhile, the unnamed black man was apprehended. While being questioned, he confessed that Ledwell and Wood had hired him to murder Ame. It was assumed at the time that Ledwell and Wood hired someone else to do the killing out of sheer cowardice. The men would have been well aware of Ame's reputation for fearlessness and ability with a gun. After the unnamed black man's statements,

Ledwell followed his cohorts in being taken into custody by local citizens.

News of the ambush and subsequent consequences was featured in multiple publications. The *Daily Democratic Statesman* of Austin cited the motive for the murder as being Wood's "exceedingly intimate" relationship with Samantha.[19] The *Galveston News* reported that after all parties had been apprehended, about thirty men gathered and took Wood, Ledwell, and the unnamed black man outside of town to where Spring Creek Road crossed Pecan Branch. All three were hanged at the same time from the same limb. Prior to the lynching, guards had been stationed at the roads leading into Iredell to prevent interference in the deed. In a *Dallas Weekly Herald* reprint of an article in the *Hillsboro Explorer*, it is written that the hanging was done from a tree that old timers described as having "a peculiarly formed limb that was shaped just right to serve as a gallows for the hanging."[20] It was also reported that a sign that read "HUNG SURE AS HELL" was carved and attached to the tree.

The three conspirators were buried at the center of the Riverside Cemetery in Iredell in unmarked graves. The still-prevalent racial tensions of the time were demonstrated by the citizenry's decision to bury the unnamed black man facing north and south as opposed to the customary east and west. Amos Smith was buried in the Martin family cemetery, which is located approximately nine miles from Iredell. It is marked only by native stone and a small tree.

Street sign at the corner of Mc Clain and Parks streets in Iredell

RIVERSIDE CEMETERY

ACCORDING TO LOCAL ORAL TRADITION, LAND FOR THIS CEMETERY AND THE ADJACENT CHURCH WAS DONATED BY THE FAMILY OF WARD KEELER, A NEW YORK NATIVE WHO CAME TO BOSQUE COUNTY ABOUT 1870 AND FOUNDED THE TOWN OF IREDELL. THE OLDEST DOCUMENTED GRAVE HERE IS THAT OF JAMES W. P. WARD, WHO DIED IN NOVEMBER 1870. THE PRIMARY BURIAL GROUND FOR IREDELL CITIZENS FOR GENERATIONS, RIVERSIDE CEMETERY CONTAINS MORE THAN ONE THOUSAND INTERMENTS, BOTH MARKED AND UNMARKED. ITS VARIED STYLES OF GRAVESTONES STAND AS A REMINDER OF THE COMMUNITY'S PIONEER HERITAGE.

4. JOSEPH THEODORE VAUGHN
1878

Joseph Theodore (J. T.) Vaughn, otherwise known to his friends as "Dorrie," was a middle-aged bachelor living on the outskirts of Bosque County in an area known as Rock School House in Hog Creek. Hog Creek is approximately six miles west of Valley Mills, Texas, along the boundary of Bosque and McLennan counties. Joseph's store and home were on the same lot of property. Joseph was well-regarded throughout the county as a trusted local merchant and banker of sorts. In a special correspondence letter sent from Meridian to the *Galveston Daily News*, Joseph is referred to as "one of the best citizens of this county."[21] It is clear that this sentiment was not an exaggeration. He was a thrifty man and rumored to have accumulated his fair share of personal wealth. In a time when banks were scarce, it was not uncommon for a trusted merchant to hold the funds of others in his personal safe. For the citizens of Bosque County, the nearest bank was thirty miles away in Waco, Texas. In addition to the considerable distance, danger of Indian attack made the trip rife with peril.

Joseph held not only the life savings of his neighbors but also a significant portion of Bosque County's governmental funds.

On June 1st, 1878, readers enjoying the much-anticipated first issue of the *Lampasas Daily Times*, read of a shocking crime. An article titled, *"BLOODY MURDER IN BOSQUE"* reported that Joseph Vaughn had been robbed and murdered at his store. The subtitle read, *"J.T. Vaughn Murdered and Robbed of Between $2500 and $2700 Four Men do the Work, for whom Hanging is Too Good."*[22] According to the article, at approximately 8 p.m. on May 28th four men had ridden onto Joseph's property and asked that he open his store so that they could purchase tobacco. As Joseph went into the store from the rear entrance, two of the men followed him inside. The men shot Joseph and robbed his store. The events surrounding the murder were revisited in a 1949 article in the *Meridian Tribune*, which featured a reprinting of an article by C. L. Douglas of the *Fort Worth Press*. Douglas had written a series on the subject of unsolved murders in Texas and in the process had come across further information regarding the night that Joseph was killed. In his article, Douglas explains that not four, but five men had arrived at Joseph's home on May 28th and asked that he open the store. Two young men, Cantrell and Lane, were inside the house when the men arrived. Reportedly, Cantrell and Lane were uneasy with the visitors and were concerned that the feud between the Horrell and Higgins families in nearby Lampasas County had just spilled over into their front yard. Out of precaution, Lane readied a cap and ball rifle while Cantrell took up arms in the form of a revolver. The young men waited in the house for signs of trouble. What they could not have known was that as they prepared for the worst, it was already happening. Two of the men were inside the store with Joseph demanding that he open his safe. The article states that Joseph resisted, not wanting to give up the $1,500 that Deputy Tax Collector Philip Nowlin had entrusted to him just the day before. It is uncertain how Douglas would have known this

27

detail. Eventually, Joseph relented and opened the safe. After emptying the safe, the men took him to the front of the store and shot him dead. Having heard the shots, Cantrell and Lane ran from the house and opened fire on Joseph's murderers. Bob Robertson, who at the time of the article was 78 years old and a retired Meridian abstractor, recalled, "I was seven years old at the time. We heard shooting at our farm home a quarter of a mile away. There were 21 shots. My sister counted them."[23]

In his autobiography, Dr. James Britton (J. B.) Cranfill gives a different account of the night of the murder. Dr. Cranfill was the son of Cranfills Gap, Texas founder Dr. George Eaton Cranfill and would have been 48 years old at the time of the murder. Dr. Cranfill makes no mention of the shootout following the attack on Joseph. He, instead, relays that Joseph had been sleeping in his store when men arrived. He states that the store was robbed and looted and further refers to the men responsible as "assassins." His word choice seems to indicate that he believed the assailants' motive was to murder Joseph, not to simply rob the safe. He also writes that Joseph's body was not found until the next day.[24] In spite of Dr. Cranfill's conflicting account of the murder, he does provide insight into the public perception of the murder at the time at which it occurred. He writes that while a man being killed in Texas was far from unheard of, it was typically the result of direct combat with another. He writes that men "met face to face, drew their revolvers, 'shot it out,' as it was called, and the trouble was over, whether one or two or half a dozen men were dead. Murder for the purposes of robbery was almost wholly unknown in those early Texas days."[25]

News of the murder of Joseph Vaughn left citizens outraged. Immediately, men from Bosque County, Coryell, and Lampasas formed a Sheriff's Posse to seek out those responsible. Sheriff Jack Cureton was undoubtedly acting just as much in the interest of the county's coffers as he was justice. While the Douglas article gives the sum of county money being held in Joseph's safe as being $1,500, the sheriff's and collections ledger from the November following the murder shows that $906.14 of county funds were stolen from Joseph's safe.[26]

The sequence of events given by the Douglas article is echoed in the *Lampasas Daily Times* and substantiated by a fatally wounded horse discovered a short distance from Joseph's property following the murder. On June 5th, 1878, the *Lampasas Daily Times* reported that they had learned from a Bosque County resident that a dead horse, along with its saddle and bridle, had been found near the scene of the murder and indicated that it died after being shot. The article goes on to say that the horse had been identified as belonging to a man who was known in Bosque County.[27] This horse would prove to be a vital clue as the hunt for the killers unfolded.

The next *Lampasas Daily Times* article in which the murder of Joseph Vaughn is mentioned was published on June 15th, 1878. The article relays the message of a mail carrier who told the paper that William Babb had been arrested for the murder. However, the author adds, "Babb is a man of wealth, and certainly has no cause to rob anyone" and promises to be watchful of further developments.[28] William "Bill" Babb was, indeed, a wealthy man. Not only did he own extensive cattle and land interest, but he owned a large general store in an area of Coryell, which he aptly named Babbville. Dr. Cranfill's autobiography goes into great detail in describing Babb. He is characterized as "one of the most picturesque characters that West Texas ever knew" and Cranfill called his store the "one of the largest general stores west of Waco."[29] Babb was not known by his business endeavors alone. Dr. Cranfill also points out that Babb routinely surrounded himself with men who were known to be some of the most daring of the western plains. Babb himself was very daring and was "feared by all of Hamilton and Coryell counties, and even as far down as Waco."[30] Babb was known to have an even temper when sober, but when drinking he often went on Dr. Cranfill described as "sprees" and would sometimes "ride his horse straight into the front doors of the Waco saloons, and at the point of his revolver, order the drinks."[31] These sprees were not merely a show of harmless bravado. After having tied one on, Babb was said to be "a daredevil, with Kit Carson, Louis Wetzel, Jesse James, Sam Bass, and Bill Babb compounded into one."[32] He and his band of cohorts had absolute run of Coryell County and no one dared oppose them. It is likely that Dr. Cranfill's knowledge of Babb is more intimate than general conjecture. David Babb, Bill Babb's brother and a Missionary Baptist minister, and Dr. Cranfill's father occasionally held revival meetings together and the families enjoyed a friendly relationship.

Bill Babb's son, Bill Ike Babb; Dave Ware; Clare Ware; and John Mayfield were arrested at Babb's ranch in Hamilton County as conspirators to the crime. Bill Babb was later arrested at his home in Coryell on June 11th, 1878. A posse numbering 300 was reported to have gone to Babb's residence to affect the arrest. The posse delivered the five men to Bosque County Jail in Meridian.[33] Bill Babb was taken in such a rush that he was not allowed to grab any money and, upon his arrival in Meridian, had to ask Captain Cureton of Meridian for a loan to feed his men. The arrest of Babb and his men was made upon a warrant sworn to by Deputy United States Marshall John Stull of Coryell County. Marshall Stull worked and resided in Coryell County in the Turnersville section. The basis upon which he was able to obtain a warrant for the arrest of Babb and his men is still uncertain, as is his actual role with the United States Marshall Service. As in the earlier case of Presley Bryant's service in the Texas Rangers, record keeping was less than ideal at the time. Other than the accounts given at the time, there are no records indicating that Stull had served as a deputy U.S. Marshall. Dr. Cranfill indicates, perhaps under the influence of his friendly relationship with Babb, that Stull harbored ill will toward Babb and that this had caused him to make the immediate assumption that Babb was responsible for Joseph's murder. Dr. Cranfill further relays that Babb and his men threatened Stull under their breaths the entire way to the jail in Meridian.[34] The only link between Babb and Joseph that was documented was mentioned in the June 18th, 1978 edition of the *Lampasas Daily Times*, which stated that the two had once been partners in a mercantile business and that they were believed to be brother Masons of the same lodge.[35]

Examining trial in the matter of whether or not to indict Babb and his men came in short order. It was reported that "Public sentiment is divided as to the guilt or innocence of the parties, some believing that there is sufficient evidence to bond them over, others confident that they will be discharged."[36] Despite Stull's best efforts to convince Judge Childress, Babb and his men were not indicted. They were released from Bosque County Jail and returned to Babbville. This would not be the last act in the saga of Bill Babb and Marshall John Stull. On December 8th, 1878, in the midst of the race to bring Joseph Vaughn's killers to justice, Dr. Cranfill received news that another murder had been committed. Dr. Cranfill and his father arrived at the Stull homestead to find the bodies of Marshall Stull and his guest, Dr. Rufus Smith. Dr. Smith, his wife, and two children were building a new home near the Stulls. Although it was coming along nicely, the chimney had not been completed. Marshall Stull gladly obliged Smith's request to spend the night in the shed so that his family could stave off the cold. Sometime in the night, the rear of Stull's home was saturated in coal oil and set ablaze. Reacting to the fire, Stull and his family ran outside. Dr. Smith, his two children in his arms, ran from the shed. The men were met by a deluge of bullets. Both were killed. Dr. Smith's wife was wounded but recovered. Although neither Mrs. Stull nor any of the children were harmed, it became evident that the individuals responsible intended to exterminate the entire Stull family when it became known that one of Stulls' young daughters had been targeted. As she hid under the kitchen table, she was fired upon. The round missed her head by only a small margin but was close enough to cut off a ringlet of her hair. Coryell County became rapt in terror. Although no one spoke of it publically, most citizens were convinced that Bill Babb was responsible for the assassination. According to Dr. Cranfill, "No one burned lights after dark unless they had impenetrable window shades."[37] Coryell County had had enough of Bill Babb. He was brought up on charges of having murdered Marshall Stull and Dr. Smith. At trial, Babb half sweet-talked and half threatened his way out of the charge. He claimed that if he and his men were allowed to leave Coryell County, the bloodshed would end. If not, it would surely worsen. The jury discussed this offer and agreed that circumventing justice was worth being rid of Babb once and for all. However, Babb did not keep up his end of the agreement and the citizens of Coryell County were not going to stand for it. A mob estimated to be 400 strong descended upon Babb's land to deliver a message. The message was that Babb could leave or he and his men would be killed. Babb left for west Texas ten days later and eventually ended up in New Mexico.

While Babb was facing his own troubles, the search for Joseph Vaughn's killers continued. Captain W. H. Glenn, a much-esteemed detective from Waco, had traced a set of horse tracks leaving the scene of Joseph's murder. He believed the tracks belonged to the horse carried two men that night. One of the men had likely arrived at the Vaughn home on the horse that was killed in the shootout. Captain Glenn followed the tracks to the home of Mart Horrell. Glenn spent the next five weeks working to apprehend his prime suspects but only succeeded in arresting one.[38] One of Horrell's men, Bill Crabtree, was placed under arrest and brought to Meridian on August 24th, 1878. Crabtree had a lengthy criminal history and a reputation as being an accomplished desperado. Several years before Joseph Vaughn's murder, Crabtree had narrowly avoided a conviction of murder in the hanging death of a man named Wallis. An article published on July 6th, 1878 in the *Lampasas Daily Times* reports an incident in which a squad of Texas Rangers set up encampment for a week or more to bring him into custody on the charge of carrying a pistol.[39] This heavy-handed approach may have been justified by Crabtree's connection to the Bill Posey Gang of McLennan County. The Bill Posey gang was a loosely-organized band of livestock thieves and outlaws. They confederated themselves under the banner of Bill Posey who, at one time, was wanted dead or alive. Appropriately, Crabtree was wanted out of Limestone County for stealing horses when he was arrested in connection with Joseph's murder.[40] For all of his blustering and bad reputation, Crabtree put up little fight when facing his second murder charge. He quickly turned state's evidence against Mart Horrell and his brother Tom Horrell. Mart and Tom Horrell were arrested and brought before Judge Childress for examination on September 8th, 1878. Captain Glenn believed that the testimony of Crabtree corroborated the circumstantial evidence against the Horrells and that a conviction was nearly guaranteed. Once Crabtree fulfilled his obligation to the state, he was allowed certain freedoms in spite of being incarcerated. One day, sometime around the 28th of November 1878, Crabtree had gone on a short walk and found himself along the banks of the Brazos River. He was ambushed and his lifeless body was left under an oak tree by unknown assailants. It was assumed that the Horrell family was responsible, yet no one was ever indicted on the crime.[41] Even with the principal witness against them dead, the Horrell brothers remained in jail. They, however, would never make it to trial.

Photo of the Old Rock School. Obtained from the Portal to Texas History

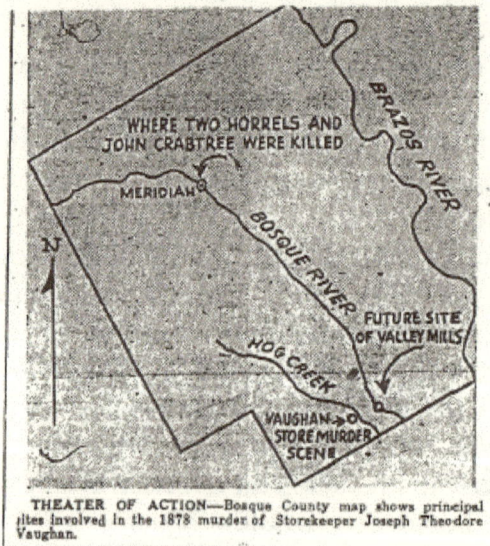

THEATER OF ACTION—Bosque County map shows principal sites involved in the 1878 murder of Storekeeper Joseph Theodore Vaughan.

Illustration from Meridian Tribune. Courtesy of The Bosque County Collection

Ledger entry showing amount of county funds taken from Vaughn safe.
Courtesy of the Bosque County Collection

Grave marker for Joseph Vaughn. Property of the Bosque County
Collection

5. MART AND TOM HORRELL
1878

The murder of Joseph Vaughn evoked disgust, fear, and anger in the citizens of Bosque and the surrounding counties. Not only had several of Vaughn's neighbors, along with the taxpayers of Bosque County, been robbed of hundreds of dollars, they had also been exposed to a type of crime rarely seen in those times. The prairie-justice circus that followed further offended the sensibilities of the populous. A favored citizen had been savagely murdered out of greed, a respected lawman had been assassinated at his home in front of his family, and the star witness of the state had been murdered in an ambush. Now, finally, after months of bloodshed, the men believed to have set it all into motion were locked away. For most of the citizens of Bosque County, there was no trial necessary. They had already decided upon the guilt of the Horrell brothers and were not going to allow another faulty administration of justice.

The Horrell brothers were undoubtedly aware of their inevitable conviction. This was not their first run-in with the law. Tom, Mart, Sam, Merritt, and Ben Horrell became known as "The lawless Horrell Boys" in 1873 in Lampasas when they shot Lampasas County Sheriff Shadrick T. Denson. Sheriff Denson was leading a posse to affect the arrest of Wash and Mark Short. The Horrells prevented the arrest by shooting Sheriff Denson, which turned his posse back on its heels. Denson would later die from his injuries. On February 10th, 1873, acting on the pleas of the Lampasas County Judge, Governor Edmund J. Davis issued a proclamation banning the carrying of side arms in Lampasas. The following month, Governor Davis sent seven members of the state police to assist in enforcing the proclamation. The state police was an asset of Governor Davis' own invention and a pet project of his administration. Following the Civil War, Texas struggled with lawlessness on the frontier. Both the Reconstructionist government that was put into place and the toppled antebellum status quo agreed that crime was rampant but could not decide upon the source of it. The Convention of 1868 reported that 939 murders had occurred in Texas since Reconstruction began just three years earlier. Sheriffs reported that from 1865 to 1871, 4,425 crimes had been reported. Of those, only 588 suspects were arrested and few were convicted. With only 82 of Texas' counties having jails, many of which were easily escapable, arresting a suspect was often pointless. With the intention to end the bloodshed, the state police was established. The new force was granted statewide jurisdiction and was placed under a central authority. It was also authorized, if not directed, to arrest those whom local lawmen either could or would not. By and large, the state police proved its effectiveness. In its three months, the state police made 978 arrests, which included 109 for murder and 130 for attempted murder. By 1872, arrest totals grew to 6,820 of which 587 were for murder and 760 for attempted murder. The Horrell brothers would have been well-aware of the power and ability of State Police Officers.[42]

On March 19th, 1873, Bill Bowen, the brother-in-law of the Horrells, was placed under arrest by the state police for defying the sidearm proclamation. The arresting officers walked him into Jerry Scott's Saloon, not realizing what awaited them inside. The Horrell brothers, along with their friends, were in the saloon and upon seeing Bowen, confronted the officers. Shots rang out, leaving four state policemen dead, including Captain Thomas Williams. After the shooting, a manhunt for the Horrell brothers began. More members of the state police, along with the new Lampasas County sheriff and the Burnet Minutemen, gave chase. Mart Horrell and several others were arrested and taken to the Georgetown, Texas jail. They would not stay there long. On May 2nd, 1873, the remaining Horrell brothers and thirty plus cowboys stormed the jail, freeing Mart and his co-detainees. The Horrell brothers remained in Lampasas County long enough to sell off some livestock before fleeing to New Mexico. They found themselves in Lincoln County, New Mexico. Lincoln County was known for its lawlessness and the Horrell brothers were soon taking part. This time, it was Ben Horrell who sparked chaos. On December 1st, 1973, Ben Horrell, former Lincoln County Sheriff Jack Gylam, and Dave Warner rode into Lincoln. The drunken men attracted the attention of Constable Juan Martinez when they began shooting their guns. Constable Martinez asked the men to surrender their weapons and, surprisingly, all three complied. The peace did not last long. A short time later, having gotten hold of more guns, the men shot up a brothel. Martinez confronted the men again, this time with four men of his own in tow. Warner, acting on a long-standing grudge against Martinez, fired the first shot; Martinez was killed. The remaining lawmen opened fire, killing Warner. Ben Horrell and Jack Gylam fled and once again found themselves being pursued. When the lawmen located the two men, they immediately began firing. Ben Horrell was shot nine times and Jack Gylam was shot thirteen. The remaining Horrell brothers, true to their nature, retaliated. They brought terror by targeting not law enforcement but two prominent Hispanic citizens. Despite the best efforts of Sheriff Alexander Hamilton Mills, the clashes continued. By the time the Horrells and their friends arrived back in Texas, they had killed at least thirteen Hispanic citizens in Lincoln and the surrounding areas.

Upon their return to Lampasas, the Horrell brothers and their confederates quickly discovered that they were no longer welcome. They were considered dangerous outlaws and some citizens went so far as to take pot shots at them. In 1876, the Horrells stood trial for the murder of Captain Thomas Williams. Miraculously, they were acquitted. More trouble was soon to follow. That same year, John Calhoun Pinkney "Pink" Higgins began accusing the Horrells of stealing his livestock. In May 1876, Higgins swore out a formal complaint upon Merritt Horrell for the theft of a calf. The case went to trial, but it did not stop Higgins from making a threat on the life of Merritt Horrell. On January 22nd, 1877, Higgins made good on his threat by shooting and killing Merritt Horrell in Wiley and Toland's Gem Saloon in Lampasas. The Horrells, again, swore revenge. It appears Higgins took action before the Horrells could, because on March 26th, Tom and Mart were ambushed about four miles east of Lampasas. Even though both were wounded, neither was killed. Higgins and another man were arrested for the attack but bonded out quickly, and on June 14th, 1877, tensions between Higgins and the Horrells came to a head. Higgins, Bob Mitchell, Bill Wren, and Higgins' brother-in-law, Bill Terry, rode into Lampasas and were met by the Horrells and their men in the town square. Despite the efforts of the citizens to dissolve the feud, an all-out gun battle erupted in the middle of town. Higgins lost three men and the Horrells lost two. After the battle, both factions fled town. Soon after, the Texas Rangers were called into town to prevent the war from rekindling. A detachment of Texas Rangers, led by Major John B. Jones, were able to peacefully arrest Tom and

Mart Horrell. Major Jones successfully negotiated a cease-fire between the warring factions. By August 1877, both sides had signed documents agreeing to end the feud.[43]

A glimmer of hope shined upon the Horrells when, in early October 1878, Judge Blackburn of Lampasas issued a bench warrant for Mart and Tom on charges pending. The nature of the charges is unknown. Judge Childress of Bosque County was not to allow this to take place. Childress remarked that he feared that the Horrells may fall victim to a mob if they were moved. However, a letter from Meridian published in the October 13th, 1878 edition of the *Galveston Daily News* reveals another potential reason for Judge Childress's refusal. Firstly, the citizens were sure that the Horrells were safe in Bosque County Jail and would be tried fairly in their courts. Secondly, it was feared that the Horrells would utilize their movement as a means of escape and they would never come to justice for their crimes.[44] Considering the Horrell brothers' history, the fears of the citizenry may have been well-founded. Sheriff James Jack Cureton was cautious of having the Horrell brothers in his jail. Fearing an angry mob intent on the undoing of the Horrells or a mob intent on releasing them, he assigned two jailers to be on duty day and night.

On Sunday, December 15th, 1878, most of Meridian's citizens were enjoying a sermon by Reverend W. D. Weir. The sermon was interrupted by gunfire. Earlier in the evening, a group of men on horseback had been seen riding around the jail as if inspecting it. They left without incident and onlookers had long since put it out of their minds. However, at around 8:30 p.m., roughly fifty masked men returned and knocked at the jail door. One of the jailers on duty, identified as Mr. Crandell, asked who was there. A man identified himself as Deputy Sheriff Whitworth. Crandell, thinking nothing of it, opened the door and found half a dozen pistols pointed at his face. He offered little resistance. When the masked men arrived at the door separating the inmate cells from the rest of the building, they encountered two additional guards. News accounts identify these two men as Messrs. Smith and Deputy Whitworth. Why Crandell would have thought that Whitworth was knocking at the door when he was already inside the building is not readily known. Deputy Whitworth and Guard Smith held the men at bay for a half hour. It was not until the men began openly discussing soaking the jail in kerosene and burning it to the ground along with everyone in it that they relented. Deputy Whitworth and Guard Smith opened the door and allowed the men inside. The men immediately went to the cells containing the Mart and Tom Horrell. Ordering another inmate to hold the light, they poured bullets into the Horrell brothers. Ed Nichols, a Meridian resident who gave a firsthand account of the massacre, recalled that Tom had run around his cell in an attempt to dodge the bullets. In contrast, Mart had stood firm, holding onto the bars of his cell doors and cursing his killers as cowards as bullets were pumped into his body. After their work was done, the men exited the jail, shouting and firing into the air triumphantly. Witness estimated the mob to be between 100 and 300 in number but stated that only fifty men were involved in the activities inside the jail. The remaining men were located in various positions around the building with the intent to keep the citizens from interfering with the dirty work inside. It is said that after the first shot rang out, Reverend Weir was preaching to empty pews. [45]

Tom and Mart Horrell's killers were never identified. The jailers on duty, perhaps truthfully and perhaps out of a sense of self-preservation, reported that the all of the men wore masks. Over the years, the guilt or innocence of the Horrell brothers has been the topic of debate, as has the identity of the men who forced their way into Bosque County Jail that night. The Horrell brothers may have been gunned down by the angry citizens they were believed to have robbed. Many believe, however, that their end came at the hands of none other than John "Pink" Higgins and his men. It has been argued that the mob could not have been comprised of angry Bosque County citizens, since most of them were attending Reverend Weir's service when the massacre began. The truth will never be known.

Courthouse Square in Lampasas Texas

Historical Marker regarding Horrell-HIggins Feud

Advertisement for the saloon in which Merritt Horrell is said to have been killed

L-R Front: Felix Castello, Jess Standard, Bob Mitchell, Pink Higgins
L-R Back: Powell Woods, Unknown, Buck Allen, Alonce Mitchell   eb001

Photo of the Higgins Gang. Obtained from Ancestry.com

6. ROBERT CONLEY
1899

Bosque County, and particularly Iredell, was considered uncivilized by the good people in Austin. Iredell's unsavory reputation may have been perpetuated by the events that followed the murder of Ame Smith. In spite of it all, Iredell continued to grow. Businesses, churches, and an additional school to combat student absenteeism sprang up. In 1880, The Texas Central Railroad arrived in Iredell and brought momentous change with it. A depot was built on the north side of the Bosque River and businesses began to pop up everywhere. Lots were sold, streets were paved, and Iredell was ushered into a new age. Newspapers all over Texas chronicled the little town's growth. Even Austin had a change of opinion. In the April 29th, 1882 edition of the Austin paper *Texas Shiftings*, Iredell was described as "having some 350 inhabitants, a half dozen general merchandise houses, one drug store, one blacksmith shop, one livery stable, two hotels, two steam cotton gins, one of the best mills, and decidedly the best school in Bosque County. Professors R. J. Richey and B. J. Word deserve credit for overcoming ... dissensions in this community ... bringing order out of chaos, and placing upon a solid basis of one of the best regulated and most progressive schools in Central Texas."[46] The first game of baseball played in Bosque County is thought to have been played in Iredell.[47]

Following the Civil War, residents of older southern states struggled in failing economies. As a result, waves of immigrants came to Texas seeing opportunity in its public lands. Iredell, with its rapid growth, attracted many. In July 1873, Francis Marion Conley, along with his wife and five children, arrived in Iredell from Georgia by covered wagon. Francis had been a quartermaster during the Civil War and, as a result of his gallantry on the battlefield, had been promoted to first lieutenant. Following their arrival in Iredell, the family grew. The second to youngest son, Robert Marion Conley, would later become a deputy sheriff.[48] Deputy Conley not only served as one of Sheriff W. A. Boyd's deputies but was qualified on November 20th, 1898 to serve as constable of Bosque County Precinct 2.[49] Just shy of five months later, on July 9th, 1899, Deputy Conley boarded the Woodmen of the World expeditionary train on the Central Texas Railway as it traveled its route from Waco. Among the passengers were Sheriff Boyd, Justice J. A. Burson of Iredell, and a fireman from Hico named Ed Burrow. The passengers were returning from the unveiling of a monument of a Woodmen of the World member. The Woodmen of the World was a benefits organization that originated in 1890 with the aim of making life insurance available to everyone. From 1890-1900, a proviso in Woodmen of the World policies included that a grave marker be provided free of charge. The original adult markers were designed as being four to five feet tall and replicated a tree trunk. Children's markers featured three stacked logs. The Woodmen of the World quickly became a fraternal organization with membership providing both practical and social benefits. While in route back from Waco, many of the passengers had become intoxicated and unruly. Some exited the train at Whitney. However, the most problematic passengers, including Ed Burrow, remained aboard. From Whitney, the train traveled to Sheriff Boyd's stop in Meridian. Prior to his exit, Boyd is credited with having kept the passengers under control. The train then continued on to Morgan heading toward Walnut Springs. During the Morgan to Walnut leg of the route, Burrow's generally disruptive behavior turned violent. While arguing with another passenger, Burrow pulled his pistol and threatened to shoot the man. Witnessing the chaos, Justice Burson attempted to take the pistol from Burrow. His attempts were not successful and he called out to Deputy Conley for assistance. Conley came into the car, drew his pistol, and told Burrow to consider himself under arrest. Burrow rushed Deputy Conley and in the ensuing struggle was able to turn Conley's pistol and place the barrel flush to the deputy's side. The weapon fired and the round entered Deputy Conley's chest just under his right nipple. As the round exited the barrel, it set Conley's clothing ablaze and burned an area about six inches wide.

As Deputy Conley lay bleeding, Burrow continued to refuse arrest or to relinquish his weapon despite Justice Burson's best efforts. Burrow, now in possession both his own pistol and Conley's, finally surrendered just before the train arrived in Walnut Springs. Burson took Burrow into custody and, upon the train's arrival in Walnut Springs, turned Burrow over to Constable H. W. Roland, who took him to Meridian and placed him in jail. The shooting took place at roughly 8:30 p.m. Deputy Conley, just 23 years old, died at 3:00 p.m. the following day. The tragedy deeply affected the citizens of Bosque County. A large audience was in attendance for Deputy Conley's funeral. Deputy Conley was buried in Riverside Cemetery and received a Woodmen of the World grave marker. The murder compelled some to call for tighter legislation on the carrying of weapons. The author of the

Meridian Tribune article that first covered Deputy Conley's murder added,

> "Can't our Legislature and our Courts do something in the way of making and executing laws that will at least check the deeds of the pistol toter? In the home, on the high way, in the courthouse and in the house of God, men and sometimes women are shot down like brutes with this deadly weapon, the pistol."[50]

Ed Burrow's trial began on February 13th, 1900. Burrow pled not guilty. He had maintained since the night of the murder that Deputy Conley had shot himself during the struggle for his gun. However, in his dying statement, Deputy Conley said, "I did not cock my pistol, not anticipating any serious trouble, he turned it on me, cocked it and shot me."[51] Burrow was deemed guilty by the jury but, oddly, not on the charge of murder. Burrows was convicted of manslaughter and received a term of confinement of only two years. The reason for Burrow being charged with manslaughter as opposed to murder may lie in revisions made to Texas statutes. In 1895, the 24th legislature adopted HB 85 resulting in major changes to the penal code. Article 698 of the 1895 version of the manslaughter statute defines manslaughter as "a voluntary homicide committed under the immediate influence of sudden passion arising from an adequate cause, but neither justified nor excused by law."[52]
Adequate cause is further defined in Article 700 as "such as would commonly produce a degree of anger, rage, resentment, or terror in a person of ordinary temper sufficient to render the mind incapable of cool reflection."[53] Article 702 goes on to list offenses that are deemed adequate cause. The list includes adultery, assault causing pain or bloodshed, great personal conflict perpetuated by violence, or insulting a female member of one's family. The offense is listed as being punishable by no

less than two years in the penitentiary and no more than five. It is unclear under which condition Deputy Conley's murder was deemed manslaughter. Many years later, Deputy Conley received the recognition of the Lost Lawman Memorial and the Officer Down Memorial Page (www.odmp.org).

According to inmate records, Ed Burrow began his prison sentence on March 1st, 1900 and was transferred to Rusk prison on March 17th. He is described as being 6' 1 ¾"tall and 170 pounds at the time of his incarceration. Oddly, he reported to the intake officer that he was temperate, in spite of having been intoxicated at the time of his offense. Although he could both read and write, his education level is listed as poor. His original release date was scheduled for February 21st, 1902. However, he was pardoned on September 30th, 1900 by Governor Joseph Sayers. He served a total of less than seven months.[54]

Woodmen of the World Picnic in Meridian, Texas. Photo was taken one month after Conley's murder. Property of The Bosque County Collection

Deputy Robert Conley. Obtained from the Officer Down Memorial Page

Conley family plot in Riverside cemetery in Iredell, Texas.

Grave marker for Robert Conley

7. JAMES AND MARY ALICE JACKSON
1902

While traveling from Shelby County, Texas in October of 1860, the William Henderson Russell family, Isaac Rundell family, and Mize family established a camp one mile east of the present location of Walnut Springs, Texas. The families established their new homestead with the 350 cattle and 25 horses they had brought with them. William H. Russell chose to settle in the Steele Creek Valley due to it being, as he put it, "a paradise for hunters, game of all kinds- birds, wild turkeys and deer, wolves and cougars – and this beautiful, hilly country with grass waving waste-high [sic] in the valleys."[55] William went on to study medicine at the Louisiana State University School of Medicine in New Orleans and in 1870, returned to Bosque County to become a beloved community physician. He was known as a typical country doctor who carried medical supplies in a pack saddle and mixed his own prescriptions by measuring them with the tip of his knife.[56] Walnut Springs was not surveyed as a town until after 1881 when the Texas Central Railroad was being brought through northern Bosque County. After the railroad's completion, Walnut Springs became the home of the headquarters of the Texas Central Railroad's divisional machine shops. A period of rapid growth followed with new settlers arriving daily. They flocked to Walnut Springs by oxen carts, horses, and sometimes on foot to seek opportunity. The hundreds of arriving families built homes and established businesses to support the railroad and its workers. Feed stores, wood shops, livery stables, meat markets, cafes, rooming houses, and, of course, saloons began to line the streets, which got their names in 1883. The town's first post office was opened in 1883 and Central College was established in 1885.[57]

James A. Jackson, along with his wife, Mary Alice, was one of the many who descended upon Walnut Springs during the early days of the railroad boom. James and Mary Alice had been married since 1875 and had their two youngest children, Stella and Flay, after they arrived in Walnut Springs. According to a letter written by Stella to and published in the *Walnut Springs Hustler*, James Jackson had been working for the railroad for eighteen years before his death in 1902. This would indicate that the Jacksons arrived in Walnut Springs around 1884. Records indicate that Stella's full name at birth was Stella Mae Jackson but was changed to Stowe when she became married. She identifies herself as Mrs. Mae Stowe. Mrs. Stowe writes that she has enclosed one dollar so that her name can be added to the newspaper's mailing list. She includes that she is a former resident of Walnut Springs but had not been there since 1905 and that Walnut Springs is very near to her heart since her father was a railroad man there before his death and it is where both of her parents are buried.[58] Since the census records for Bosque County from 1890 were destroyed by fire, the timeframe the Jacksons arrived cannot be confirmed. However, James, Mary Alice, Stella Mae, and Flay appear on the census accounting for Bosque County in 1900.

In December of 1901, Mary Alice was taken before the

county judge on a charge of lunacy. She was determined to be insane and sent to the asylum. She did not remain there for long. James, convinced that his wife was cured, went to the asylum and had her released in February or March of 1902. In the first weeks of Mary Alice being home, she appeared to be doing well. However, other members of the Jackson family were soon to become less sure of her recovery. An unnamed son of James and Mary Alice was reported to have urged James to return Mary Alice to the asylum out of fear that she may harm the two youngest children who were about twelve and fourteen years old at the time. It soon became clear that James should have heeded his son's caution.

On April 22nd, 1902, James returned from the railroad sometime after midnight. He was a hustler at the Texas Central roundhouse and was typically kept well into the night by the arrival of late trains. On this particular night, he went home and was asleep shortly after. According to Mary Alice's confession, she got out of bed sometime between five and six in the morning and retrieved an axe. She struck him on his head so forcefully with the axe that his skull was nearly split in two. He lay in bed, evidently still breathing but not conscious, until he died at about 7 a.m. She stated that she had brutally murdered her husband because he "treated her so mean."[59] That same day, she was brought to Meridian by Constable Rowland and delivered to jail authorities. She was to be kept confined until Sheriff Little received instructions from the asylum as to what was to be done with her.

The citizens of Walnut Springs were shocked by the crime and saddened by James' murder. They described him as "one of the most quiet and peaceable men in the town"[60] and contended that any mistreatment Mary Alice experienced from James must have been entirely imaginary on her part. The general consensus was that Mary Alice had relapsed into insanity and killed her husband. After all, according to the *Meridian Tribune* her actions could not be "accepted as any other than that of an insane person."[61]

By Wednesday, April 23rd, Sheriff Little had received the instructions for which he had been waiting. He was told that Mary Alice had only been released from the asylum on furlough and that she was to be returned immediately. The next morning, she told Deputy Sheriff Randall that she badly wanted to see her children and apologize to them before she was sent away. Deputy Randall reported that she seemed to be rational and genuinely remorseful for her actions and saw no fault in allowing her to deliver the message. Randall then left her cell, presumably to make arrangements for the children to visit. When he returned a short time later, Mary Alice was hanging from the top of her cell wall. She had torn her undergarments to pieces and used them to construct a rope. Randall immediately recognized that Mary Alice was choking to death and rushed into the cell to cut her down. She fell to the floor and Randall thought she was surely dead. He called for the jail physician but could not reach him. Instead, Dr. J. J. Lumpkin was called and arrived at the jail shortly after. He was able to resuscitate Mary Alice, but she did not speak or even regain consciousness. Much like her husband, she laid unconscious but breathing until 11 p.m. when she died. A second doctor, A. F. Lumpkin, determined the cause of death to be inflammation of the brain and spinal cord. James and Mary Alice Jackson are buried at Oak Grove Cemetery in Walnut Springs, Texas.

Downtown Walnut Springs, Texas. Property of the Bosque County Collection

Walnut Springs, Texas Trade Days circa 1900. Property of the Bosque County Collection

Walnut Spring rail yard. Property of The Bosque Collection

Walnut Springs railroad mechanics. Property of The Bosque Collection

One of Texas Central Railroad's remaining rail road bridges in Walnut Springs

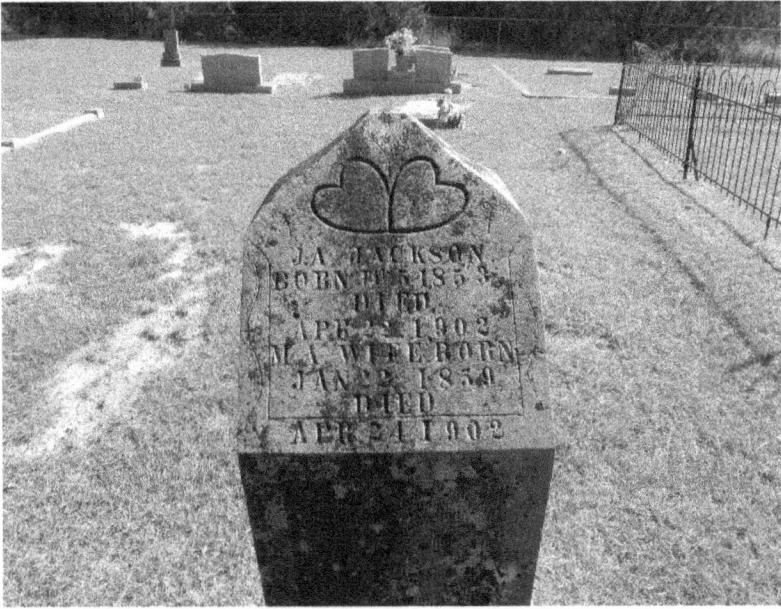

Grave marker for James and Mary Alice Jackson. Surprisingly, they are buried together

8. THE ETHRIDGE CHILDREN
1913

In 1847, well before Bosque County's formal establishment, the State of Texas granted eighteen labors (a Spanish land unit measuring 177 acres) of land along Childress Creek to James Smith, who, in turn, deeded roughly 3,300 acres of the land to James Pinkney Henderson on March 8th, 1852 at the cost of $2,000. Henderson had served as the first Governor of Texas from 1846 to 1847 and was a former Major General in the U.S. Army. Governor Henderson died in 1858, leaving the property to his wife and daughters. The daughters conveyed their share of the land to their mother, who arranged to have it sold in 1877. The center of the property once owned by Governor Henderson lies seven miles northeast of Clifton. In 1879, the population of the settlement and the surrounding area was roughly 200. Hugh S. Anderson, who owned and operated a general store in the area, applied to have a post office established. Hugh was successful and the post office opened on January 8th, 1880. On February 25th of the same year, the community was formally named Womack after the man who would become the town's first postmaster, Thomas Womack. The Womack Post Office was in operation until its discontinuance in 1906. The area was largely open with stock animals roaming freely. Womack enjoyed a large influx of German settlers; in fact, the area was so decidedly German that religious services and classes at the local school were commonly conducted in German. As late as 1920, it was not uncommon for a Womack child to have never encountered the English language until going to school. Some of the first generation German settlers had received a few years of instruction in English. However, most of them learned it on their own.[62]

Clarisa Ellen Walker was born to Samuel Houston Walker and Celia Fishburn Walker on September 29th, 1866. She grew up in a home of little means along with her older brothers, Sam and William, and younger sisters, Mattie and Charlotte. In the written recollections of an unknown family member, she is often referred to as Clara. However, she will be remembered for her misdeeds as Ellen Ethridge.

In written recollections, Ellen is described as being "slightly retarded" and a "poor, uneducated soul." Family members recall Ellen's discomfort with being poor by noting that on the few occasions she attended school, she would trade an entire lunch for a biscuit, which she would bring home to share with her sisters. Ellen's lunches typically consisted of fatback and cornbread, and it was widely held, at the time, that the poor ate cornbread while the more affluent ate white bread or biscuits.[63] On March 23rd, 1893, Ellen married the first of what is believed to be four husbands. Charles West was a widower with three children. Little is known of the nature of this union, other than it produced a daughter, Allie. It is, however, likely that it was not the heat of passion that brought the two together. Ellen was 27 years old when she first married. In 1893, being unmarried and close to thirty threatened a life of spinsterhood. Her appearance may have also been a factor.

Very few photos exist of Ellen. However, she was described as being of "short, stout build" with "heavy, dull features."[64] Charles, left wifeless with three children, surely needed someone to care for them and his household. Charles passed away when Allie was three or four years old. Allie followed him in death at the age of eight.[65] The cause of these two deaths is still unknown but would certainly be called into question in the latter months of 1913.

Years later, Ellen's younger sister Mattie married S. S. Malone. Malone was a tenant farmer on the Looney Ranch (also known as the Fitzhugh Ranch). It was through Malone that Ellen met another tenant farmer on Looney Ranch named James (Jim) D. Ethridge.[66] It was said of Jim that he was "one of the highest types of tenant farmers and holds the respect of the entire community, and stands well wherever he is known."[67] He had nine children, to whom he was quite devoted. In late 1912, Jim's first wife fell ill from the birth of her ninth child and Ellen became her sole attendant. The reasons for this arrangement are unclear. The first Mrs. Ethridge died in January of 1913. Oddly, the physician responsible for her care declared that she had "every hope of recovery" on what would be his last visit with her.[68] It is believed that she died shortly after the physician left her bedside. In March of 1913, Ellen became the second wife of Jim Ethridge and the mother to his children.

Signs of trouble began to show three short months later. Eight of the nine Ethridge children were left in the care of Ellen. The infant had been sent to the care of Jim's brother. In June of 1913, the family physician, Dr. Coston of Womack, was summoned to the Ethridge household. Beulah, two years old, and Harrison, ten years old, were violently ill. Upon Dr. Coston's arrival, Ellen suggested that she thought the children were suffering from diphtheria.[69] Diphtheria, a bacterial infection of the upper respiratory tract, was a common and devastating illness at the time. Epidemics of deadly illness such as diphtheria, flu, and small pox had swept Bosque County, taking the lives of far too many children in years past. Sadly, both children died. Dr. Coston, however, was unsatisfied with the explanation provided by Ellen but lacked sufficient information to launch a formal investigation into the children's' deaths. Jim must have been devastated at the loss of his children. The *Meridian Tribune* said of Jim that he "was a very loving father and so devoted to his children that he never allowed them to want for anything within his power to give them."[70] It would not be long until tragedy once again touched his family. On the morning of October 2nd, 1913, Jim was out tending to his work on the ranch, as was undoubtedly his routine. Ellen was at home alone with four of the children. One of the children was a thirteen-year-old who was not named, the others were Oscar, age five; Dick, age nine; and Pearl, age seven. According the account of the thirteen-year-old, the three younger children had been sent to put a letter in the rural route box, which was approximately a half-mile from the home. All three returned around 11:30 a.m. The children were tired when they returned and were given a snack of buttermilk and cornbread by Ellen. Shortly thereafter, the rest of the family, with the exception of Jim, convened for the noon meal. Within half an hour after the meal, the three youngest children became horribly ill. The first to show signs of distress was little Oscar. He began to complain of abdominal pain and nausea. Dick and Pearl followed him in short order, experiencing the same exact symptoms. Dr. Coston was once again called to the home. When Dr. Coston arrived, he found the children writhing in pain, and, perhaps acting on his earlier suspicions, he immediately began administering emetics and other remedies that were common in treating poisoning. Dick and Oscar were beyond any hope of help and died within four hours of leaving the dinner table. Pearl, miraculously, made a full recovery. Pearl later told investigators that she was not very hungry upon returning from her trip to the post box and did not drink much of her milk. She may have saved her own life. [71]

Dr. Coston's immediate assessment that the children were victims of poisoning, along with the similar nature of the deaths of the other two Ethridge children, set into motion a searching investigation. Sheriff H. W. Randal, County Attorney H. S. Dillard, and County Health Officer J. Frank McDonald arrived at the Looney Ranch and were followed by Justice of the Peace T. J. Rhodes. When Ellen was asked if she knew how the children may have been poisoned, she answered that she had thought they were suffering from indigestion caused by apples they had eaten earlier in the day. Sheriff Randal, clearly disbelieving her answer, began to search the home for any kind of poison. While searching a trunk that "was under lock and key" in Ellen's bedroom, Sheriff Randal noticed Ellen take an old hand satchel that had been tied with a handkerchief and wrapped in a towel from the trunk. It appeared to Sheriff Randal that Ellen was trying to conceal it beneath the bed covers. Sheriff Randal examined the satchel and found inside a package containing a whitish powder. When questioned, Ellen insisted that the powder was medicinal salts that had been given to her by her mother. Dr. McDonald was certain it was not salts in the package. Ellen appeared dumbfounded and emphatically denied any wrongdoing. Her demeanor changed once the package was confiscated. Accounts state that she became "indifferent and refuse[d] to talk further than to deny knowledge of the cause of the death of the boys."[72] Ellen's deadly web was closing in around her. It is assumed that upon leaving the residence, Dr. McDonald took custody of the whitish powder and the boys' bodies. He is cited as having had the responsibility of delivering the stomachs and livers from their little bodies to Baylor Laboratory in Waco for analysis by analytical chemist Professor Samuel R. Spencer. As of the initial reporting of Ellen's arrest, which came approximately three days later, Professor Spencer had already determined that the whitish powder found in Ellen's bedroom contained 75%

arsenic. Ellen was arrested as a result of these findings. Even after Ellen was placed in Bosque County Jail, her husband firmly believed his wife to be innocent. Local law enforcement and media, however, were far less trusting. It was initially reported that the analysis of the stomachs and livers of the boys did not show signs of arsenic poisoning. Professor Spencer, presumably along with Sheriff Randal, was so sure the children had been poisoned that he planned to send a portion of the children's' spinal columns or brains to the Baylor Laboratory if the second analysis did not render evidence of arsenic. There was a correction a week later in the *Meridian Tribune* stating that the first analysis had, indeed, rendered positive results for arsenic but that a second test was conducted for verification. The local media also focused attention on Ellen's past. The cause of death of Ellen's first husband and their child, as well as the late Mrs. Ethridge, were called into question so much so that County Attorney Dillard was rumored to ask commissioner's approval to have the late Mrs. Ethridge's body exhumed.[73] There is no record of the exhumation ever having taken place.

On the Saturday following her arrest, Ellen Ethridge "made her first statement that showed any signs of her weakening." Throughout the initial inquest and on into her stay at the Bosque County Jail she staunchly declared no wrongdoing. That is, until she was faced with Professor Spencer's findings. Upon hearing the findings, she stated, "Man ought to be as charitable as God."[74] Shortly thereafter, she gave full confession of her crimes. Her lengthy written confession gives little indication of motive. The confession does, however, give precious insight into her mindset at the time of the murders. Ellen mentions that on the morning that she poisoned the first two children, she had a headache and the youngest child, Beulah, was worrying her. The child tugged on her dress for attention, and Ellen fed her lye for it. Harrison worried her as well. Ellen gave him lye twice, once, it seemed,

69

just on a whim. Ingestion of the documented causes burns in the esophagus and excruciating abdominal pain. The children would have died in agony. Oscar, Dick, and Pearl had done nothing but come in wet after an errand Ellen herself had sent them to complete. Ellen wrote in her confession:

> "They were wet when they got back from being out in the rain, and they looked like they were going to be sick from the exposure to the bad weather, and I thought they would be better off dead than alive."

The question this statement poses is if she meant that the children would be better off dead than sick or if she would be better off with them dead as opposed to having to care for sick children. Surprisingly, a special session for grand jury was not called to settle Ellen's case. In spite of her full and chillingly cold confession, she was expected to plead not guilty by reason of insanity. During the week of December 19th, 1913, Ellen Ethridge went to trial at Bosque County courthouse for the first of her four murder charges. The first trial was in the matter of Oscar. As expected, Ellen pled not guilty by reason of insanity. At trial, the few people who knew Ellen well testified on her behalf. Each witness called testified that he regarded Ellen as an "idiot." In 1913, the term idiot was used to describe someone who so mentally insufficient as to not be able to care for themselves. Attorney Dillard, however, had a different take on Ellen's mental state. He contended at trial that Ellen was "insanely jealous of the children" because her husband gave them too much attention and neglected her and that she "planned to remove them, after she had brooded for a long time over her imaginary woes."[75] The jury found Dillard's theory of the case more plausible and handed down a guilty verdict within an hour. Ellen was given a life sentence. She elected to plead guilty to the remaining charges and received four life terms, as well as an additional five years for her attempt on Pearl's life. Media outlets had different perspectives on Ellen's behavior in court.

The *Waco Time-Herald* characterized her as being "without the least trace of emotion" as the verdict was read. The *Meridian Tribune* was a bit less harsh, saying that "she paid no attention to the court proceedings, but since the trial has been greatly affected."[76] Jim Ethridge was present throughout the trial.

At the time of the Ethridge children's deaths, it was typical to bury lost loved ones on family land. Jim Ethridge, unfortunately, did not own any land of his own outright. The owners of the Looney Ranch donated a small section of property upon which the children would be buried. It is now known as Womack Cemetery and has fallen into a state of disrepair over the years.

Prison records indicate that Ellen was sent to Huntsville to begin her sentence on December 31st, 1913 and moved Camp Goree (also known as the Goree Farm or the Goree Unit) the same day. She was released on furlough on October 27th, 1927 and voluntarily returned to Goree on January 23rd, 1928. She was made trustee on June 12th, 1929.[77] Family letters indicate that she spent her time as trustee freely roaming the prison grounds. She also sold jams, as well as lace pillowcases that she knitted for those who came to visit other inmates. She had very few visitors of her own. Upon her release on January 18th, 1932, she moved to an unnamed state and died in a nursing home on July 14th, 1947 at the age of 81.[78]

Cemetery believed to contain the unmarked graves of the Ethridge children

9. WILLIAM T. HIX
1914

John J. Smith, along with his wife and seven of his ten children, arrived in Bosque County, Texas from Scott County, Mississippi around the mid-1850s. He and his family settled in a bend along the Bosque River about twenty miles east of Meridian. He built a double log home not far from the gin that he used to care for the cotton he raised on several hundred acres. His son Jeff served in the Civil War and, upon returning home in 1868, hauled lumber from east Texas to build his home, complete with two rock fireplaces. Jeff took to raising fine racehorses and held races around the county. Jeff's younger brother Gip gave land and built the area's first school and church. The area came to be known as Smith Bend. As the turn of the century neared, Gip continued building. He constructed houses, a general store, a new modern gin, and dug three artesian wells. Roswell, as the town was named, became the post office of the Smith Bend area. The outlying areas of Smith Bend were inhabited primarily by tenant farmers. A blacksmith's shop came along, providing a gathering place for the community's men, along with the barbershop.[79] Smith Bend was, however, not without its problems. As the town was growing, so was its population and as is often the case, neighbors did not always get along.

William T. Hix first appears on the Bosque County census in 1900. Previous records show that he lived in both Erath and Hill counties prior to settling in Smith Bend. It is clear that Hix arrived in Bosque County sometime between 1880 and 1899 and immediately set about making a name for himself. According to an article that ran in the November 24th, 1899 edition of the *Houston Daily Post*, Hix had been having troubles with two of his renters. The two men, identified as Jno. Crum and James Kirkpatrick, were engaged in a sharecropping arrangement with Hix. The arrangement turned sour in November when Hix disagreed with his renters over the corn crop that would be used to pay Crum and Kirkpatrick's rent on the land. The dispute became so heated that neither side wanted the other to gather the crop until the matter was settled. On November 21st, 1899, Hix sent word for Kirkpatrick and Crum to come to his residence and fetch his wagon and team so that they could gather the corn. When the men arrived at roughly one o'clock in the afternoon, Hix asked how they intended to haul the corn and Crum said that they would haul it load for load – one load for Hix and one load for themselves. According to the article, Hix responded by saying, "That's business boys." Around roughly the same time, two men returned to the residence from the crib. It can be assumed from later documentation that the two men were Hix's son, Boyd, and a man named Joe Spivy. Hix then began to ask why Kirkpatrick and Crum had been saying that they had intended to whip him and his boys. This sparked an argument. The article does not explicitly state who shot Kirkpatrick and Crum but instead only says that both a shotgun and a pistol were used to shoot them both dead. Crum and Kirkpatrick were both armed at the time of the shooting but only Crum was able to draw his weapon and fire. The round did not find a target. [80] Hix surrendered to deputies the same day.

In early January 1900, William and Boyd Hix, as well as Joe Spivy, bonded out of jail. The same article shows that Laura Bell Kirkpatrick, James Kirkpatrick's widow, filed civil suit against William Hix for killing her husband.[81] William and Boyd would be indicted for murder the week of January 26th. [82] Spivy was not indicted. The case was set for trial in mid-February but delayed due to the trial of Ed Burrow for the murder of Deputy Robert Conley.[83] Hix would not go to trial for the murders of Kirkpatrick and Crum until January 1901, when he pled guilty to manslaughter. He was sentenced to time in the penitentiary in February 1901 but only served a few years before he was pardoned and returned to Smith Bend. Having murdered Kirkpatrick and Crum earned Hix a reputation for being a man who was not afraid to carry out a threat. This reputation would eventually become his undoing.

In June of 1914, William Hix was not in the better graces of James Bryan and his sons. Hix had, according to contemporary reporting, been making threats against Fred, John, and Bill Bryan. Although there was rumor of a "patch up" among the men, it soon became clear that not all wounds had healed. The *Meridian Tribune* featured dueling versions of the events, which occurred on June 7th, 1914, but both articles agree on some facts. On the morning of June 7th, Hix rode to the property of Mr. Ford where Ford and his hands were cutting oats. Ford's property was across the road from the home of Fred Bryan. The other Bryan boys, John and Bill, were at Fred's house at the time. After Hix shared a meal with the Fords, the Ford boys mounted a horse and buggy and started back down to the pasture with Hix following them on his horse. As the group neared the main road, which passed Fred Bryan's house and led to Hix's house, shots rang out from the direction of Fred Bryan's house. The horse drawing the Ford boys was spooked by the shots and ran out of control. The Ford boys reported seeing John Bryan with a gun, continuously firing at Hix. They also reported that Bill and Fred Bryan were standing in the road with their guns firing at Hix as well. The top of Hix's head was blown off and it was reported that his brains were scattered for several feet through a barbed wire fence.

Further details differ from one reporting to the next. The first account, which was released on June 12th, states that the initial shots spooked Hix's horse as well, and the animal ran out of control toward the pasture gate, approximately two hundred yards from the Bryan house. It is reported that the Ford boys saw Hix opening the gate as Bill and Fred fired upon him. It is also reported that Hix was unarmed at the time of the shooting and did not even have a weapon in his saddle pocket.[84] An article published on June 19th paints quite a different picture. The article, furnished to the *Meridian Tribune* by J. P. Word (defense council for the Bryans), details continuous threats made by Hix against the Bryans. It makes clear that Hix had threatened to kill the Bryans and had, two or three times, gone to John Bryan's home, armed with both a pistol and shotgun for the purpose of making good on his threat. It also points out that having a meal with the Fords was the "pretended purpose" of him being in the area. John Bryan is reported as having gone back to his residence to attend his stock but, knowing Hix was in the area, decided to take his shotgun with him when he returned to Fred's home. While on his way back to Fred's house, John saw Hix was going to pass between his brother's and his house. Fearing the worst, John stopped and held his gun down behind him, thinking that Hix would not see him or the gun and would pass by without incident. As Hix saw John, he cursed him and reached down toward his saddle pocket as if reaching for a gun. John fired on Hix. When Fred and Bill heard the shots, they looked down the road to see Hix riding toward the pasture gate at a trot but could not see their brother. They assumed Hix had shot and killed John and ran down toward the gate to help him. Fred and Bill saw Hix around the pasture gate and they, too, reported seeing Hix reach for his saddle pocket. Being of the same mind as their brother, they both fired upon Hix, in defense of themselves and their brother. The account ends by reminding the reader of Hix's previous prison sentence for manslaughter and adds that "Hix was considered a man who would carry out any threat that he might make, and thus ends the life of another man who dug who own grave by his conduct."[85]

On the day of the murder, J. P. Word, Sheriff H. W. Randal, and H. S. Dillard attended the scene. The men spent the night in the community and returned to Meridian with the Bryans in custody the following day. The Bryans waved examining trial in favor of having bonds set immediately. They bonded out for $10,000 each and returned home to await indictment. John went to trial for the first time during the week of September 25th, 1914. After an unsuccessful attempt by defense council to have the indictment set aside, the case was continued due to the absence of several key witnesses. Ultimately, the Bryan brothers pled guilty to a reduced charge of manslaughter and were sentenced to two years in the penitentiary.

William Hix and Family. Courtesy of the Hix family

Extended Hix family and friends. Believed to have been taken after William Hix's funeral

10. EDNA HELEN KELLERSBERGER
1923

After the City of Kent failed, another settlement began to emerge roughly two miles south of its location. The Kimball Township was formally established in 1853-1854 by Richard B. Kimball of New York. Kimball acquired the land as part of his and Jacob Raphael de Cordova's colonization arrangement and was located roughly eighteen miles Northeast of Meridian. De Cordova was a Jamaican-born printer by trade but soon discovered he had a knack for following the flow of money. De Cordova's ties to Texas began in 1836 when he traveled to New Orleans. There, he shipped cargoes of staples to Texas during its struggle for independence. Following the battle of San Jacinto, he visited the Republic of Texas in support of an organization to which he had ties. He remained in Texas and settled in Galveston in 1839. After moving to Houston, he was elected as a State Representative to the Second Texas Legislature in 1847. He only served one term. During his time in office, de Cordova traveled the Texas frontier extensively. He purchased large amounts of land through either direct purchase or scrip and resold them to settlers. At one time, it is estimated that he had a million acres in scrip or title. In a bid to attract buyers for his land, he gave speeches all over the country, including New York.[86] It can be assumed that he came to be acquainted with Richard Kimball on one such trip. The original town of Kimball was surveyed close to Kimball's crossing, which at the time was one of the few crossing points of the Brazos River. The first Kimball post office was opened in 1860. The Kimball Academy, in the downtown area, began to hold classes in 1873. By 1884, Kimball was home to a variety of business, including gristmills, cotton gins, two hotels, stores, and shipping houses for agricultural products.[87] Kimball's early successes can be attributed to its location on the Chisholm Trail. A major route out of Texas for livestock, the Chisholm Trail provided a steady source of income that helped impoverished Texas recover from the Civil War. After the war, one of Texas's only potential sources of revenue was its countless Longhorn cattle, for which there was no market. Due to the Texas fever carried by Texas Longhorns, Missouri and Kansas had closed their borders to Texas cattle in the 1850s. In the spring of 1867, Joseph G. McCoy persuaded Kansas Pacific officials to law a siding in Abilene, Kansas, on the edge of the quarantine area. This effectively opened up the market to Texas cattlemen.[88] Kimball's decline began when the large cattle drives on the Chisholm Trail slowed to a trickle. It, however, was the community being bypassed by the railroad in 1881 that sealed Kimball's fate. From that point forward, the population steadily decreased.[89]

Philip Bosche and his wife, Nora, moved to their 3,000-acre farm in Kimball shortly after their marriage in 1921. Phillip, a wealthy businessman, owned the Bosche Building in Austin, Texas where Nora, then known as Nora Combs, ran a photography studio. At the time of their marriage, Nora was forty and Philip was 61. In 1919, before marrying Nora, Philip had taken a considerable financial loss when oil deals he had made in association with former Texas Governor William Pettus Hobby and his brother, Edwin Hobby, flopped. In response to the crisis, Philip deeded all of his property to his adult children. His daughter, Edna, was deeded the Bosche Building in Austin as well as a farm Philip owned on the Colorado River. Her older sister, Winifred, was deeded the Kimball Bend Plantation. It can be assumed that this decision was made to protect the properties in the event of another financial crisis.

Marital bliss was short-lived for the newly-wed Mr. and Mrs. Bosche. Shortly after their marriage, Nora filed for divorce and attempted to have the property, already deeded to Philip's daughters, divided as alimony. Her efforts failed. Shortly thereafter, Nora dropped her divorce suit and the couple was reunited. Within months, they would separate again. This time, the division was at the bequest of Philip Bosche. In July of 1923, Philip filed for divorce in the district court of Bosque County after having discovered Nora with another man in his home one night in June. Upon seeing the two together, Philip grabbed a shotgun and fired upon them. Contemporary news reports state that Nora and her clandestine lover were only slightly wounded "on account of the gun being loaded with birdshot."[90] After the incident, both Nora and her lover were charged with adultery. The man promptly plead guilty and paid his fine. Nora was arrested on the charge but promptly bonded out. As of October 1923, her charges were still pending. As part of the divorce proceedings, Philip obtained an injunction prohibiting Nora from entering the Kimball Bend Farm. Nora moved to Dallas. She made one final effort to come home when she wrote a letter to her attorney, Will R. Parker of Fort Worth, asking him to get her permission from District Judge Irwin T. Ward visit the home she had shared with her estranged husband. Judge Ward permitted the visit under the condition Nora obtain permission from Philip. Nora made her request, to which Philip responded in writing, "No, I won't take you back. I have my daughter at the farm and we are getting along nicely. I don't want you to bother me."[91] Later that day, Nora went to Fort Worth and boarded a train bound for Kopperl, Texas.

In mid-October 1923, Philip's youngest daughter, Edna, and her two young daughters arrived at the Kimball Bend Farm to visit Philip and assist him in household manners. Edna, now a bride herself, had married a Methodist Missionary Dr. E. R. Kellersburger, who was stationed in Africa. Edna had served alongside her husband until she contracted "sleeping sickness" a year earlier. African sleeping sickness, or Trypanosomiasis, is a vector-borne parasitic disease that is spread when a host is bitten by the tsetse fly. It only occurs in 36 sub-Saharan African Counties and is considered fatal. One of the disease's most notable epidemics began in 1920; Edna was one of its victims. Upon falling ill, she was sent to London where she remained in the hospital for seven months before returning to America. Her husband choose to stay in Africa and continue his work. On October 23rd, 1923, Edna and her two- and six-year-old daughters were preparing breakfast at the Kimball Bend Farm while Philip's brother, Matt, was out feeding the stock. Philip was in Dallas attending the fair. Unknown to Edna, her stepmother was in the backyard of the residence, where she had been hiding since she walked there from Kopperl the night before. Nora slipped into the kitchen through the rear door. According to the Edna's oldest daughter, Winifred, Nora told Edna, "You know what you have done. I am going to kill you" as she walked into the kitchen. Edna responded, "Let me explain." Before Edna could finish her sentence, Nora fired a 25 caliber automatic pistol at her. The round missed and lodged into the ceiling. Edna tried to run for the front door, but Nora fired again. This time, the round entered through Edna's hand and abdomen before coming to rest in her spinal column. She fell to the floor. Nora grabbed the shotgun that her husband had fired at her four months earlier before fleeing the home. Matt, who heard nothing, was alerted by the children's screams. He rushed to the house where he found Edna bleeding to death by the front door. He picked her up and placed her on the bed where she died shortly after. According to witnesses, Nora came across a tenant of the property roughly 300 yards from the house. She told the man, "I killed a woman who ruined my home" and continued walking to William Cleveland's residence. Sheriff W. W. Wright and Deputy C. A. Barker were called and responded to Cleveland's home where they placed Edna under arrest. [92]

Upon arriving in Meridian, Nora waived examining trial and refused to give a statement. Justice of the Peace Enos Jenkins denied her bond. Even as Nora sat in jail for the murder, the men in Edna's life remained unaware of her death. Her father had heard a man being called out for on the loud speaker at the Dallas fair with the announcement that his wife had been killed. Philip never considered that the announcement was inaccurate and actually meant for him. He did not discover that his daughter had been murdered until the next morning when he read of it in a Dallas newspaper. Edna's husband could not be reached due to a lack of telegraphic communication in the African Congo. He would not hear of his wife's murder for an estimated 90 days.[93]

Nora was indicted for murder on December 3rd, 1923 and her trial was set for December 27th.[94] However, her trial was delayed due to the absence of Edna's husband. She was granted bail at that time in the sum of $7,500[95] but did not secure her release until January 12th, 1924 when M. Coniglio and J. M. King of Fort Worth posted her bond.[96] Her trial date was set for March 31st. On the day of the trial, Nora was not in attendance. Her attorney requested a continuance on the grounds of Nora having had an operation on March 23rd that rendered her unable to travel. He even provided a signed affidavit from her Oklahoma City physician. District Judge Irwin Ward denied the motion for continuance and ordered

Nora's bond revoked. She was to be brought immediately back to Meridian and the men who signed for her bond would forfeit the bond amount. Deputy Sheriff Barker was sent to Oklahoma City to investigate Nora's absence and bring her back to Meridian. He first spoke with Nora's doctor. For reasons unknown, the physician's medical opinion changed as he spoke to Deputy Barker. He agreed that Nora was fit for travel. A short time later, Barker found Nora in a hotel and informed her of the court's decision. She agreed to return to Meridian with the deputy.[97]

Nora finally went to trial in April of 1924. Testimony began with Dr. J. H. Burnett's testimony that he was called to the residence to tend to Edna but that she was already dead of a gunshot wound upon his arrival. Next came the testimony of Steve Hughes, the night agent at the Kopperl train station. He testified that Nora had arrived from Fort Worth on the 11:25 train on October 22nd, the night before the murder. There was also a bit of controversy as County Attorney Anderson was denied the opportunity to share with the court a statement that Nora made to him before her arrest. Shockingly, the prosecution's star witness turned out to be little Winifred. She told the court of Nora's entry through the rear door of the house and how an unarmed Edna tried to talk to Nora but was shot instead. At one point during her testimony, the little girl pointed at Nora and stated, "That is the woman that killed my mother."[98] Nora had her own version of the events. She testified that she had spoken to her estranged husband in Dallas on October 22nd. According to Nora, Philip had brought two boxes of dishes to her and afterward they had a brief conversation in which he told her to go back home to the Kimball farm. She stated that she boarded the train to Kopperl that night and arrived at 12:30. She then walked about seven miles to the farm from the station because her husband had told her that he did not want the neighbors to know she was home. She arrived at the farm at daylight and went to the front door of the home but found it locked. She then went to the rear kitchen door and entered. According to her testimony, when Nora entered the kitchen she was confronted by Edna, who was holding a knife and told her "You and I can't stay here together." Nora attempted to reason with her stepdaughter, telling her, "You are welcome to stay." Nora stated that she did not finish her sentence before Edna rushed her with the butcher knife. Nora took a pistol from her pocket and fired over Edna's head with no intention of harming her. Nora then went toward the front door, when she turned and realized Edna had grabbed her father's shotgun and was pointing it at her. Nora fired to prevent Edna from shooting her. Nora stated that she did not recall anything beyond that point until she left the house. She did, however, remember picking up the shotgun from near Edna's body and taking it with her for protection. She also stated that she had seen Mr. Hadley while walking to Mr. Cleveland's residence but could not recall what she said to him. Nora was careful to point out that she did not go to the house with malice. She had only taken the pistol for protection, since she had bought it from a pawnshop the previous August for that purpose. Oddly, she had purchased the weapon under her maiden name, Nora Combs. She also stated that she had very little contact with the victim other than having taken her picture when she was still working as a photographer in Austin. There were also two letters presented during Nora's testimony. One was written by Nora to a friend in which she shared how happy she and Philip were together. The other was written by Nora to Edna on May 23rd, 1923, which discussed Edna's disapproval of her father's marriage to Nora. Nora insisted, however, that Edna had done nothing to break up her home.

There were witnesses to provide testimony that refuted much of what Nora had said to the court. Firstly, a search for weapons had been conducted on the day of the murder and none were found. An old knife was found in a pan on the shelf in the back room but did not match the description Nora gave of a butcher knife. As a matter of fact, Mrs. E. E. Dixon testified that she had been at the residence very close to the time of the murder and helped prepare dinner and that she had to use a pocketknife to cut meat due to there being no butcher knife available. J. G. Hadley testified that when he spoke to Nora as she left the property, Nora stated, "I got the woman that broke up my home and am now going to tell the Sheriff to come and get me."[99] In front of a packed courtroom, the jury found Nora Bosche guilty of murder and sentenced her to 20 years in the penitentiary.

Nora was first sent to Dallas to await transport to Huntsville. Prison records show that she arrived in Huntsville on April 20th, 1924 and was transferred to Goree State Farm for Women on the same day. Her inmate record reflects that she was 5' 3 ½" inches tall and 114 pounds with a fair complexion, dark brown eyes, and brown hair. She also had a gold crown on an upper left tooth and scars on the left side of her face, back of her neck, and lower part of her back. She was noted as being a Christian and wearing a size four shoe. She was able to read and write but had only had seven years of schooling.[100] She made her first attempt at obtaining a pardon in January of 1927 when H. B. McAllister of Waco traveled to Huntsville to gather letters of recommendation from prison officials that he could deliver to Governor Miriam A. Ferguson. At that time, she is described as being "practically an invalid, having clubfeet, and is in very poor health. She is a first class prisoner and never breaks the rules having a clear record."[101] Although prison records do not reflect Nora being of poor health, her status as a model prisoner is supported by her being made trustee on August 10th, 1928.[102] Nora's second bid for clemency came in 1929. This time, Nora had a particularly pressing reason for securing her freedom. She had met a man named G. Lewis Harrington, who was incarcerated in the Huntsville Unit, and intended to marry him. In July 1929, Nora told a Huntsville reporter that she and Lewis had met when the prison-sanctioned band he was a member of came to play at the women's unit. She relayed romantically of how they had visited under a chinaberry tree and were immediately attracted to each other. She described Lewis as being a native of England who spoke seven languages, a college graduate, an accountant, and an undertaker. The couple met again when Prison General Manager Colonel W. H. Mead's wife asked Nora to come and sew for her. Nora claimed that the Colonel and his wife were sympathetic of their affair and allowed Lewis to come out and see Nora at their residence without a guard. She went on to claim that Colonel Mead told her that she and Lewis were free to have their wedding at his home. Nora had secured a wedding dress and gotten the matron of the farm, Mrs. Reid, to take her into Huntsville to get a permanent wave. She believed that once she was released, she and Lewis would move to south France and start a new life.

Lewis completed his sentence and was released on June 29th, 1929. Upon his release, he met with Nora's son Arthur and went to Austin to try to secure Nora's pardon.[103] Despite Senator Julian P. Hyer's promise that he would do all he could to obtain her parole, Governor Moody turned a deaf ear. Despite the setback, Nora and Lewis were married on July 26th, 1929 at Goree Farm. Oddly, the couple did not wed under their legal names. Instead, they took their vows under the monikers J. L. Morrison and Lenora Bell Combs. Morrison explained the name changes by saying, "The names Harrington and Nora Bosche are dead as far as we are concerned. They never were our names."[104] The ceremony was officiated by Reverend W. E. Miller, the prison chaplain. Not everyone was in agreement with the nuptials. Captain G. W. Reid, manager of the Goree farm, did not attend the wedding, stating, "I want the people of Texas to know that I am not in sympathy with such a wedding. I do not approve of such a thing, for the penitentiary is no place for weddings, but is for punishment and reform."[105] Nora

Bosche/Lenora Combs was released from prison on December 22nd, 1932.

Men working along the Chisolm Trail. Property of The Bosque County
Collection

90345

[FORM FOR NATIVE CITIZEN.]

DEPARTMENT OF STATE
PASS PORT

No. SEP 14 1920

Issued ISSUED
WASHINGTON

UNITED STATES OF AMERICA.

STATE OF **North Carolina**

COUNTY OF **Mecklenburg** } *ss.*

I, **Edna Bosche Kellersberger**, a NATIVE AND LOYAL CITIZEN OF THE UNITED STATES, hereby apply to the Department of State, at Washington, for a passport **for myself and 3year old daughter, Winifred Helen Kellersberger.**

I solemnly swear that I was born at **New Philadelphia**, in the State of **Ohio**, on or about the **6** day of **August**, **1886**; that my ~~father~~ | husband **Eugene R.Kellersberger**, was born in **Cypress Mill, Texas** and is now residing at **Concord, North Carolina**

that I have resided outside the United States at the following places for the following periods:
Belgian Congo from **Oct. 21, 1916** to **Feb. 2, 1920**

and that I am domiciled in the United States, my permanent residence being at **Concord** in the State of **North Carolina**, where I follow the occupation of **Missionary on Furlough** My last passport was obtained from **Department of State**, on **Oct.2,1916** and was **cancelled** [Disposition of passport.] am about to go abroad temporarily, and I intend to return to the United States within **One** with the purpose of residing and performing the duties of citizenship therein; and I desire a passport for use in visiting the countries hereinafter named for the following purpose:

England & Belgium [Name of country.] — **En route to Belgian Congo** [Object of visit.]
France and [Name of country.] — **Enroute** [Object of visit.]
Switzerland — **Visit relatives**
Belgian Congo [Name of country.] — **Missionary** [Object of visit.]

I intend to leave the United States from the port of **New York, N.Y.** [Port of departure.]
sailing on board the ____ [Name of vessel.] on about **December 15**, 1920. [Date of departure.]

OATH OF ALLEGIANCE.

Further, I do solemnly swear that I will support and defend the Constitution of the United States against all enemies, foreign and domestic; that I will bear true faith and allegiance to the same; and that I take this obligation freely, without any mental reservation or purpose of evasion: So help me God.

Edna Bosche Kellersberger
[Signature of applicant.]

Sworn to before me this **9** day
FEE REC. SEP 1 3 1920
[SEAL OF COURT.] of **September**, 1920.
C. B. Fetzer

Deputy Clerk of the **U.S. District** Court at **Charlotte, N.C.**

4472

Customs record of Edna Kellersberger's reentry into the United States following her illness

Age: 33 years. Mouth: Medium

Stature: 5 feet, 6 inches, Eng. Chin: Prominent

Forehead: Medium Hair: Dark Brown

Eyes: Gray Complexion: Dark

Nose: Short Face: Narrow.

Distinguishing marks: None

IDENTIFICATION.

September 9, 1920

I, H. L. Smith, solemnly swear that I am a { native } citizen of the United States; that I reside at Charlotte, N.C.; that I have known the above-named Edna Boscha Kellersberger personally for 4 months and know her to be a native citizen of the United States; and that the facts stated in her affidavit are true to the best of my knowledge and belief.

H. L. Smith

Com'l Sup't Sou. Bell Tel. Co.
(Occupation.)
Charlotte, N.C.
(Address of witness.)

Sworn to before me this 9 day

of September 1920

[SEAL]

C B Fetner

Deputy Clerk of the U.S. District Court at Charlotte, N.C.

Applicant desires passport to be sent to the following address:

135 S. Union st.,

Concord, N.C.

m. f.

A signed duplicate of the photograph to be attached hereto must be sent to the Department with the application, to be affixed to the passport with an impression of the Department's seal.

Following page of Customs record including photo of Edna Kellersberger and her daughter

11. MENLOE JERMSTAD
1936

As the Great Depression reaped havoc across the nation, Bosque County was not spared. When residents of the City of Clifton were required to register if in need of assistance in March of 1933, 107 residents applied. Much like other cities nationwide, work, as well as hope, was scarce. President Franklin Roosevelt acted swiftly to try to curb joblessness by enacting "The New Deal." Under Roosevelt's initiative, government-funded public works projects were started across the county in order to gainfully employ as many as possible. The Works Progress Administration, or WPA, ultimately employed 8.5 million people at an average salary of $41.57 a month. Workers built bridges, roads, parks, airports, and all other manner of public infrastructure. Just days after citizens of Clifton stood in line, shamed and broken, more than half were employed on a WPA project clearing the Clifton Municipal Park.[106] In 1935, Meridian received funding for its WPA project. A sum of $12,425.60 was allotted to construct 25,882 linear feet of sidewalks throughout the city of Meridian. That November, forty men began working on the project.[107] One of those men was Menloe Jermstad.

Menloe was born in Bosque County on January 27th, 1907. He was a farmer by trade but joined the WPA rolls to help overcome financial hardship. The toll the Great Depression took on his family was devastating. Menloe's father, brother, and uncle had committed suicide out of the shame and fear caused by financial ruin. He and his bride, Clomer Allen-Jermstad, had only married in 1928 and he was no doubt feeling the pressure of providing for his family. Menloe often fell to fits of despondency and feared that the "curse" of his family would find its way to him. Shortly before Menloe began work on the WPA project, it is said that friends and neighbors had become concerned he would succumb to the pressure and follow his family's dark tradition into death. Clomer was a 5' 4", brown haired, brown-eyed, born and raised Bosque County native. She was Baptist and reasonably educated for the time, having completed six years of formal schooling, and could both read and write. She was described as a buxom and attractive woman. Menloe often spoke in glowing terms of his wife's beauty and devotion.

Sometime around the beginning of 1936, the couple struck up an agreement with a tenant farmer named George Pace on the Stockard Farm. While George and Menloe were out looking for odd jobs, Clomer was to keep the house for the men. George and Clomer had known each other nearly all of their lives and had been an item in their youth. Clomer and George described themselves as school-yard sweethearts, while Menloe and George described themselves as best friends. It was an awkward mixture at best. In a turn of events that was hardly surprising, an affair began between Clomer and George shortly after Clomer and her husband moved in. Clomer's family soon became suspicious of the living arrangements and persuaded the couple to move out. By all accounts, it seems that Menloe was blissfully ignorant to the betrayal occurring before him.

Throughout the affair, Clomer outwardly remained a faithful wife, giving her husband no reason to suspect any misdeed. Clomer and George left the Stockard Farm and moved into a ramshackle cabin owned by Clomer's uncle, Matt Allen. The cabin was on sandy soil and located just outside of Meridian.

On April 24th, 1936, Clomer got out of bed early to prepare breakfast for her husband, as was her routine. As they sat together, enjoying the meal, Menloe spoke cheerfully of his days as a WPA employee. He also told his wife of an attack he had suffered at work some days before. According to the men on the job site, Menloe had experienced pain and shortness of breath, which he attributed to some trouble with his heart. He told the story almost jokingly, having long gotten over his concern about the event. As he finished his meal, he took his first large gulp of coffee and immediately began exhibiting signs of difficulty. According to a manuscript submitted to the popular crime magazine *Inside Detective* by Sheriff Pearl Benson and published by the magazine in November 1937, Menloe's body became rigid and the color drained from his face. He gasped "My Heart!" and doubled over in excruciating pain. Clomer let out a scream that alerted Matt Allen to the trouble. When Matt witnessed Menloe's horrifying state, he ordered Clomer out to get a doctor.

When Dr. J. S. Calhoun arrived, Menloe was laying on the bed surrounded by neighbors and friends. Dr. Calhoun pushed through the crowd to evaluate his patient. Menloe's eyes were glazed and half-closed. One hand dangled on the floor and the fingers were curled into a claw-like shape. There was no doubting that Menloe was dead. Clomer told the doctor that Menloe had just had one of the attacks he had told her about. Dr. Calhoun asked if he had been ill, to which Clomer replied no. Calhoun returned to the body and opened one of Menloe's eyes. He noted that the pupil was narrowed to a pin point and that the capillaries of the eyeball were congested. This led Calhoun to initially believe that Menloe had been strangled to death. Calhoun also noted that Menloe's muscles were already rigid with the early onset of rigor mortis, which he found puzzling. As the doctor left the house, Matt was the first to ask the question on everyone's mind: Did Menloe commit suicide? Due to his melancholy as of late and family history, it was natural to assume that Menloe had inflicted his own death. Dr. Calhoun, however, sincerely doubted it. He returned to town immediately and summoned Sheriff Pearl Benson.

Sheriff Benson wrote that in spite of having been ill for several days, he was overtaken by curiosity and suspicion regarding Menloe's death. It was his curiosity that compelled him to leave immediately for the little cabin. Benson, Dr. Carroll, County Attorney S. C. Smith, Justice of the Peace E. H. Young, and Deputy J.C. Royal began their inquest at once. As they questioned witnesses, the two prevailing theories became clear. The locals to the area had at once adopted the suicide theory, while Menloe's coworker's at the WPA project assumed that he must have succumbed to a heart ailment. As the rest of the men continued with their questioning, Sheriff Benson began a rather covert examination of the kitchen where Menloe had spent his final moments. Immediately, his eye was drawn to a small bottle which bore the label "strychnine." Benson wondered why a family with a history of suicide and a noticeably despondent husband would have such a large quantity of a potent poison. Benson reached out and took the bottle into his hand. To his surprise, it was empty. After having made such a startling discovery, Sheriff Benson went to find Dr. Carroll. Once the two men were outside, Benson told Carroll of his discovery and asked him if he thought Menloe could have died of strychnine poisoning. Dr. Carroll told him that while such a poisoning would explain Menloe's peculiar post mortem systems, he could not be sure without an examination of Menloe's viscera. Sheriff Benson ordered that the examination be conducted immediately.

Deputy Royal and P. H. Benson Jr. took the viscera from

Menloe's body to Waco the following morning for analysis by Baylor University chemist, Dr. W. T. Gooch. By Monday morning, Dr. Gooch had made his preliminary report that the viscera, indeed, contained strychnine. Gooch concluded that a large enough dose of strychnine remained in Menloe's stomach alone to kill a man. Justice Young rendered an inquest verdict that Menloe's death was caused by poisoning. For some, Dr. Gooch's findings only solidified the theory that Menloe had taken his own life. After all, he was plagued by "the black things," as evil emotions were called in the area, and he had access to the poison determined to have killed him. Sheriff Benson, however, remained unconvinced. He believed that Menloe, having just obtained a new job, would not have been in ill enough spirit to take his own life, much less with a substance that caused such an agonizing death.

Working on his theory alone, Benson returned to the Jermstad home. When he arrived, no one else was there. He was hot, so he walked down a wooded path to the spring and, after drinking from it, retraced his steps back to the house. Halfway up the path, he stopped dead in his tracks. He could see, across the tops of the bushes, a small glade sheltered by trees. Thinking it the ideal resting place, he walked closer. Before having even left the path, Sheriff Benson could see a number of white cigarette stubs in the grass. This confirmed his suspicion that someone had been spending large amounts of time there. He pushed through the bushes and entered the glade, immediately realizing that this was no ordinary resting place. The grass had been pushed down in such a way that made it apparent that not one, but two people had been lying there for long period of time. This place had been, as Sheriff Benson would later write, "a sylvan bower of love – a trysting place for two lovers!"[108] Sheriff Benson knew that he had just made a monumental breakthrough in the case but that he would have to tread lightly in proving it. He decided to go back into town and make a few discreet inquiries.

He learned, right away, that many people had seen a couple, though they could not identify who, going in and around the wooded spot. It was not until Sheriff Benson spoke to members of a railroad section crew who worked in the area that he got the first confirmation of his suspicions. A man told him that he surely recognized the couple that had been hanging around the woods; it was the Jermstad woman and the man that worked at the Stockard Farm. This discovery fueled Sheriff Benson and led him to question many others in pursuit of the truth. He found that not only had Clomer and George been longtime lovers, but George was planning on marrying Clomer before she was swept away by the handsome Menloe. The final piece of the puzzle fell into place when the farmer who supervised George on the Stockard Farm told Benson that George had been gone all night the night before the murder. All that was left to do was to put the poison in George's hand. Knowing that drug stores kept accounts, called poison books, of those who bought substances such as strychnine, Sheriff Benson went to Turner's Drug in Meridian to see who all had purchased strychnine around the time of the murder. He found that someone calling himself Arthur had bought twenty cents worth of the poison on the Tuesday before Menloe's death. Sheriff Benson asked the druggist if he knew Arthur, as the name was unfamiliar to him. The druggist answered that the man who called himself Arthur lived just a little way outside of Meridian but insisted that the Sheriff knew him. The druggist had seen the Sheriff speaking to "Arthur" on the street.

Benson, determined that George Pace and the mysterious "Arthur" were one in the same, instructed Deputy Royal and his son, P. H. Benson Jr., to bring Pace in for questioning under the guise of wanting to ask him if Menloe had experienced any heart spells while living with him on the Stockard Farm. George initially could not be found, but the men left word for him to come and speak to the sheriff. Thinking that George would be eager to come in and answer questions, Sheriff

Benson instructed his son to stay in Turner's Drug and wait for his signal. As expected, George produced himself in short order. When he arrived, he immediately began telling Sheriff Benson of the numerous attacks Menloe had while living at the Stockard Farm. According to his article in *Inside Detective,* the Sheriff said, "I guess you've been having a gad heart attack yourself," to which George fidgeted uneasily and replied, "Well, Sheriff, I guess you've been young once yourself."[109] With this, Benson stepped into front of the open drug store window and signaled his son by tossing a rolled up newspaper into the street. In a few moments, Benson Jr. brought the druggist to the door. Sheriff Benson asked if he knew the fellow standing beside him and the druggist replied, "Sure. Hello, Arthur." George immediately began cursing the druggist and denying ever having presented himself as Arthur. There was no more need for discretion on Sheriff Benson's part. He went to work on George. He confronted him with the affair, the meeting place in the woods, and the strychnine. George initially denied everything until the Sheriff informed him that Clomer had been determined to be in the clear and that he would be taking the blame for everything. In a momentary loss of composure, George shouted, "Like Hell she is! She's in just as deep as I am." With that, George knew that had made a damning mistake. He sat down sullenly and refused to speak further without a lawyer. However, after nearly an hour of reminders from Sheriff Benson that the first one between him and Clomer to tell the truth would likely get some sort of leniency, he made a full confession.

With George now locked away in the county jail, Sheriff Benson set out to find George's co-conspirator. Benson went back to speak with Clomer, took her to an area where he believed she and George had met the night before, and informed her that George had confessed. Although Clomer agreed that George's story was true, she was quick to point out that the two had met someplace else. Clomer was also placed in

Bosque County Jail. At examining trial, Justice Young ordered them both remanded without bail.

During their stay in jail, confessions were obtained from both parties. In his confession, George stated that the plot to kill Menloe began approximately one week before the Jermstads moved out of George's home. He stated that he and Clomer agreed that they would get rid of Menloe but had not yet agreed upon the method. After the couple moved out, Clomer and George continued to meet frequently and, during one of those meetings, agreed that they should poison Menloe. The Tuesday before Menloe's death, George purchased strychnine and gave it to Clomer that night in a secret meeting. The two met again on the following night and agreed that Clomer would administer it the following morning.

Clomer's confession states that roughly a week before moving out of George's house, she and George had decided to marry if they could get rid of Menloe. Though divorce was discussed as an option, Clomer "did not want her husband here on earth if she married another man."[110] She corroborated George's claim that they continued to meet frequently after she and her husband moved and that George gave her the strychnine in one such meeting. This is, however, where the lovers' stories begin differ. Clomer stated that George was very eager to see Menloe done away with. As a matter of fact, Clomer claims that George begged her to give her husband the poison at the first available opportunity. When they met on the night after the poison exchange, George was distraught that Clomer had not yet killed Menloe and threatened to kill him himself if she did not administer the poison soon. She claims they then discussed how best to give him the poison and first discussed putting it in cocoa before deciding upon putting it in his coffee. Clomer confessed that at approximately 5:30 a.m. on April 24th, as she prepared breakfast, she poured the contents of the small bottle of strychnine into the coffee cup intended for Menloe. She waited until she could hear him coming to the table before pouring his coffee on top of it. He took the first swallow and complained that the coffee was bitter, so Clomer poured out the remaining coffee and refilled his pot with her coffee. She had already thrown the empty strychnine bottle into the cook stove. Within minutes, Menloe began complaining of hurting or cramping and asked Clomer to send for a doctor. As she was leaving to walk to a neighbor named Will Martin's residence, Matt Allen came in. Instead of contacting Martin, she came upon Ben Neal and asked him to go into town for a doctor. Instead of watching her husband die, she waited at Martin's home. By the time she returned, Menloe was dead. Dr. Calhoun arrived shortly after.[111]

During the week of September 18th, 1936, the Grand Jury indicted Clomer and George on murder charges.[112] Trial was set for September 30th.[113] Clomer's trial came first. In Judge O. B. Mcpherson's court, she pled not guilty. The defense attempted to prove that Menloe's death was self-inflicted and that Clomer was of weak mind and did not know right from wrong. Ultimately, Clomer's confession was far too damning. In less than an hour, the jury delivered a guilty verdict and she was sentenced to 45 years in prison.[114] George Pace's trial came immediately after. George also entered a plea of not guilty; however, his was on the bases of insanity. Upon hearing George's defense, Judge McPherson ordered that he first be given a lunacy trial. For reasons unknown, George's attorney, W. F. Myers of Fort Worth, waived the lunacy trail in favor of proceeding with the matter at hand. The defense presented evidence indicating that George's mind was defective due to childhood disease. They contended that due to his mental defect, he did not know right from wrong and was acting under the influence of Clomer Jermstad. Witnesses were also called to the stand to testify to George's morose and peculiar disposition since having suffered typhoid fever several years back. The witnesses believed that George's mind had been weak since the illness. The prosecution presented testimony by

Sheriff Benson, Matt Allen, County Attorney S.C. Smith, and, of course, George's confession. George was determined to be guilty of being an accomplice to the murder of Menloe Jermstad and sentenced to 75 years in prison. Once the verdict was rendered, Meyers filed a motion for a new trial, which was quickly overruled. However, because of Meyers' insistence that his client was insane, Judge McPherson deferred sentence to allow Dr. Ben Turner, Johnson County Health Officer, to observe George.[115] Clomer, too, filed a motion for a new trial. Neither would have their sentences vacated.

Clomer Jermstad entered the Goree Unit by way of Huntsville on October 14th, 1936. Prison records list her formal charge as murder with malice. She appears to have been designated as trustee on May 20th, 1937 and received the first of several reprieves on January 24th, 1940. At that time, she was granted reprieve by Governor O'Daniel. On April 9th, 1943, she received a 90 day reprieve from Governor Stevenson and was to report to Honorable Tom Parke, the chair of the Bosque County Parole Board. This particular reprieve was extended first by six months and then by a year. She received a conditional pardon on November 14th, 1945, followed by a full pardon on January 26th, 1948.[116] Upon release, she returned to Meridian where she died in 1982.

George Pace began his sentence at Huntsville on July 3rd, 1937 on the charge of Accomplice to Murder with Malice. He was quickly transferred to Harlem Camp #1 on July 10th, 1937 and back to Huntsville in October of the same year. He also enjoyed lengthy reprieves starting in May of 1945. He received conditional pardon on July 2nd, 1952 and full pardon on May 17th, 1963, along with restoration of his civil rights. George also returned to Meridian and died in 1981.[117]

HAUNTED BY FOREBODINGS
Menloe Jermstad and his wife Clomer seemed happy with their children when this picture was snapped. But Jermstad lived under a constant cloud of fear. . . .

Menloe Jermstad along with Wife Clomer and Children. Photo provided to *Inside Detective* magazine by Sheriff Pearl Benson

ACCUSED POISON MURDER PAIR IN BOSQUE JAIL

Sheriff Pearl Benson (center) with George Pace and Mrs. Clomer Jermstad, in Bosque county jail. The couple are charged with the murder of the woman's husband, Monloe Jermstad.

Front page photo from the May 1st, 1936 edition of the *Meridian Tribune*

Sheriff Pearl Benson. Courtesy of the Jeff Hightower family

Turner Drug Store. Property of The Bosque County Collection

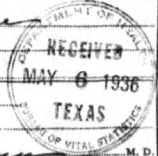

Menloe Jermstad Death Certificate

Grave marker for Menloe Jermstad and other Jermstad family members.
Found in historic St. Olaf cemetery in Cranfills Gap, Texas

Grave of George Pace

12. FRANK AND DAVID HORNBUCKLE
1941-1942

Richard Franklin Hornbuckle brought his wife, Emeline, and children, William, Sarah, Francis, Wiley, Franklin, Amanda, and Alice, from Marshall, Alabama to Cherokee, Texas sometime between 1853 and 1860. Franklin was listed as being seven years old on the 1860 census. Franklin, or Frank as he would be known, later moved to Bosque County and appeared on census records there in 1900. He settled about two miles west of Morgan, Texas with his wife, Malinda, and their children, as well as their niece. Two years later, Frank would become the sheriff of Bosque County. He remained in office until 1908. His service as sheriff and long history in the county established him as one of the "county's oldest and best known citizens."[118] Understandably, the citizens of Bosque County were shocked when, on October 21st, 1941, Frank was shot dead by his own daughter, Addie.

Addie Hornbuckle was born in 1888 while the family was living in Cherokee, in San Saba County, Texas. Census records from 1940 indicate that Addie lived with her mother and father. She was 53 years old, never married, and unemployed, despite having completed two years of college. The census indicates that she had other income sources, although it is unclear what those sources were.[119] It was initially reported that on October 21st, 1941, Addie had walked into Morgan at approximately 4:00 p.m. She remained in Morgan until 7:30 p.m. when she contacted Charlie Hornbuckle to take her home. When Charlie and Addie arrived at the Hornbuckle residence about thirty minutes later, they found Frank Hornbuckle in outside near the back door of the residence. He was dead of gunshot wounds. It was indicated that he had been dead for several hours. Once law enforcement arrived, it was determined that Frank had been shot twice with a rifle. One round appeared to have entered his left side near his heart and the other entered in his left arm. Addie was immediately placed under arrest and taken to Meridian. Her examining trial was held the same day. Justice of the Peace Will Ligon set her bond at $5,000. Bond was made and she was released. [120]

Addie was indicted for murder in March of 1942 and trial was set for April 6th.[121] As the trial neared, there was an assumption that the trail would be continued due to the hospitalization of two material witnesses. Dr. C. C. Cate was in the hospital in Houston and Addie's brother, David Preston Hornbuckle, was in the hospital in Meridian. It was thought that the defense counsel would request a change of venue in the event that a motion for continuance was granted.[122] No such motion was granted and 175 jurors were questioned for suitability before settling upon twelve men from Clifton and Valley Mills. Citizens from all over the county were in attendance as District Attorney Gene Turner and County Attorney Paul Massey began direct testimony with Judge B. F. Word presiding.[123] The trial went on for six days. Addie testified that the gun fired accidentally. Contemporary reports do not indicate how she explained Frank having been shot twice nor is any explanation given regarding Addie's "discovery" of Frank's body several hours later. After eighteen hours of deliberation, the jury found Addie guilty of murder without malice. She was sentenced to two years, which were suspended. She served no prison time for Frank's death.[124]

In October of 1942, the Hornbuckle family was at the center of tragedy and controversy yet again. David Preston Hornbuckle, former Bosque County Tax Collector and son of Frank Hornbuckle, was found dead of a pistol shot wound to the chest on October 1st, 1942. It was just over a year after the eerily similar death of his father. At approximately 10 p.m. on October 1st, David's son Howard reported to Sheriff David Montgomery that there were "two dead people"[125] at David's residence near five miles north of Meridian. Sheriff Montgomery, Constable Tom Gillaspie, and Highway Patrolman E. F. Vantreers arrived at the scene to find David dead and his wife, Mary Alice, near death with a similar pistol shot wound. Mary Alice was immediately taken to the hospital in Clifton, Texas. Howard was arrested in light of statements given to investigating officers while on scene. Witnesses from the area indicated that Howard had demanded that David, who had been an invalid for four years, deed the family ranch to him. Although Mary Alice agreed to the transfer, David refused. Howard then drew a .22 target pistol and shot them both. It was also noted that Howard had been committed by Bosque County to the State Psychopathic Hospital in Galveston on April 24th, 1942 for 90 days of treatment and observation. He was released from the hospital in June at the request of Mary Alice. Contemporary sources indicate that he was not shown to have been formally discharged.[126] Howard waived examining trial and was held without bail for David's murder. Curiously, no charges were filed for the assault on Mary Alice.

Howard's brother, T. C., immediately began fighting to have Howard's competency questioned. T. C. Hornbuckle filed a lunacy charge on Howard on October 17th. The charge was heard in Bosque County Court on October 20th but was dismissed due to the Court's involvement in Howard's criminal charges. The Court cited jurisdictional issues as the grounds for dismissal.[127] As expected, upon the case being called to trial in December of 1942, an affidavit was filed alleging that Howard was insane. B. F. Word, who had sat as judge for Frank Horbuckle's trial, was Howard's defense counsel. In light of the filing, the Court ordered that evidence to be submitted on the issue. A total of twenty witnesses, including four doctors, testified to Howard's insanity. Upon conclusion of the trial, jurors were instructed to answer the following questions:

No. 1: Do you find from the preponderance of the evidence that Howard Hornbuckle was insane at that time he shot and killed his father?

The jury answered no.

No. 2: Do you find from a preponderance of the evidence that Howard Hornbuckle is insane at this time?

The jury answered yes.

No 3: If you have answered the above Special Issue No. 2 in the affirmative then answer the following question:
Do you find from the preponderance of the evidence that Howard Hornbuckle should be confined in an institution for the insane?

The jury answered yes.[128]

On the decision of the jury, the Court ordered that Howard be sent to the State Hospital for the Insane and that if he were to be determined sane by hospital staff at any time, he be returned to the sheriff of Bosque County to stand trial for murder. There is no record of any such trial having ever occurred. Mary Alice Hornbuckle made a full recovery from her wounds and later moved to Dublin, Texas where she died on November 13th, 1957. Howard died in Llano, Texas on March 8th, 1984. The family is buried in Meridian Cemetery.

Photo taken inside Turner's Drug Store in Meridian, Texas. Preston Hornbuckle is identified as being marked with the number 4 in the photo. Obtained from The Portal To Texas History

Frank Hornbuckle Death Certificate

1. PLACE OF DEATH
STATE OF TEXAS
COUNTY OF *Bosque*
CITY OR PRECINCT NO. *Meridian*

2. FULL NAME OF DECEASED *David Presto Hornbuckle*

LENGTH OF RESIDENCE WHERE DEATH OCCURRED *50* YEARS — MONTHS — DAYS (SOCIAL SECURITY NO)
RESIDENCE OF DECEASED STREET AND NO. CITY *Meridian* COUNTY *Bosque* STATE *Tex*

PERSONAL AND STATISTICAL PARTICULARS

3. *Male*	4. COLOR OR RACE *White*
5. SINGLE, MARRIED, WIDOWED OR DIVORCED (WRITE THE WORD) *Married*	
6. DATE OF BIRTH *Mar. 10, 1888*	
7. AGE *53* YEARS *10* MONTHS *21* DAYS IF LESS THAN 1 DAY HOURS — MIN —	
8A. TRADE, PROFESSION OR KIND OF WORK DONE *Ranching*	
8B. INDUSTRY OR BUSINESS IN WHICH ENGAGED	
9. BIRTHPLACE (STATE OR COUNTRY) *Texas*	
10. NAME *Marion Frank Hornbuckle* (FATHER)	
11. BIRTHPLACE (STATE OR COUNTRY) *Texas*	
12. MAIDEN NAME *Matilda Abbott* (MOTHER)	
13. BIRTHPLACE (STATE OR COUNTRY) *Texas*	
14. SIGNATURE (INFORMANT) *Mrs. Troy Baxter*	
ADDRESS *Dublin* TEXAS	
15. PLACE OF BURIAL OR REMOVAL *Meridian* TEXAS DATE *October 4* 194_	
16. SIGNATURE (UNDERTAKER) ADDRESS *Meridian* TEXAS	
20. FILE NUMBER FILE DATE *Oct 7 194_* SIGNATURE OF LOCAL REGISTRAR *W.W. Wright* POSTOFFICE ADDRESS *Meridian* TEXAS	

MEDICAL PARTICULARS

17. DATE OF DEATH *10/1* 1942

18. I HEREBY CERTIFY THAT I ATTENDED THE DECEASED FROM *Dec. 1938* 194_ TO *Oct. 1* 1942
I LAST SAW H— ALIVE ON *Oct. 4* 1942
THE DEATH OCCURRED ON THE DATE STATED ABOVE AT *10* *P* M.

THE PRIMARY CAUSE OF DEATH WAS: *Gunshot wound in chest* DURATION

CONTRIBUTORY CAUSES WERE —

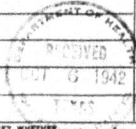

IF NOT DUE TO DISEASE, SPECIFY WHETHER ACCIDENT, SUICIDE, OR HOMICIDE *accidental h—*
DATE OF OCCURRENCE *10/1/42*
PLACE OF OCCURRENCE *Meridian, Texas*
MANNER OR MEANS *Bullet wound*
IF RELATED TO OCCUPATION OF DECEASED, SPECIFY *none*
SIGNATURE *R.D. Holt* M.D.
ADDRESS *Meridian* TEXAS

David Preston Hornbuckle Death Certificate

Hornbuckle Graves

HISTORICAL MAPS

Bosque County 1855
Property of The Bosque County Collection

Bosque County 1869
Property of The Bosque County Collection

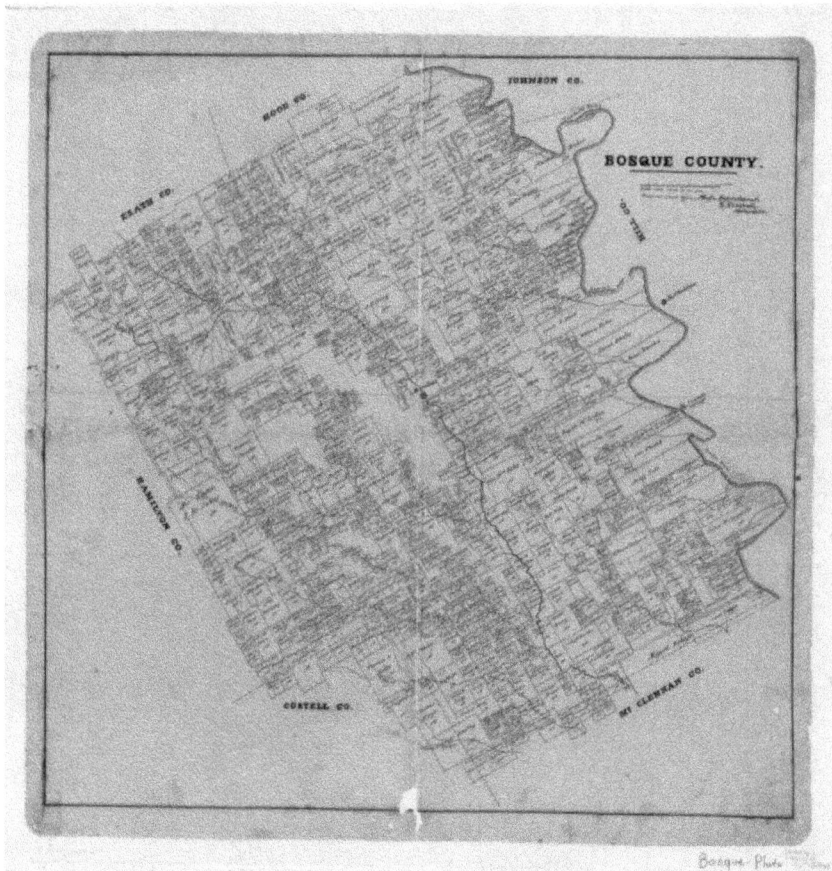

Bosque County 1871
Property of The Bosque County Collection

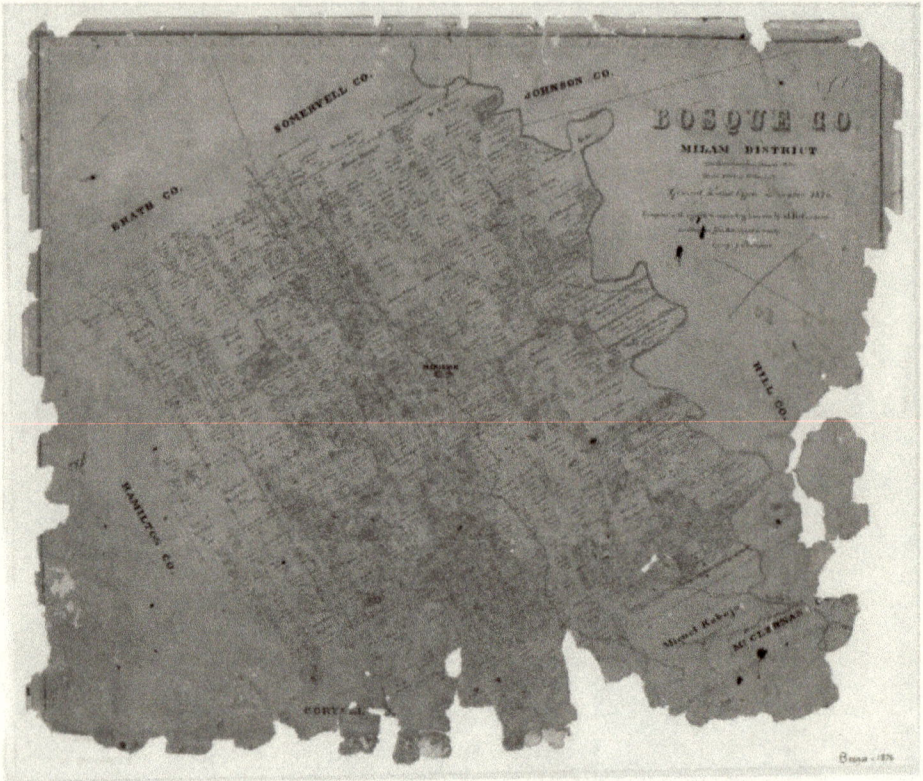

Bosque County 1876
Property of The Bosque Collection

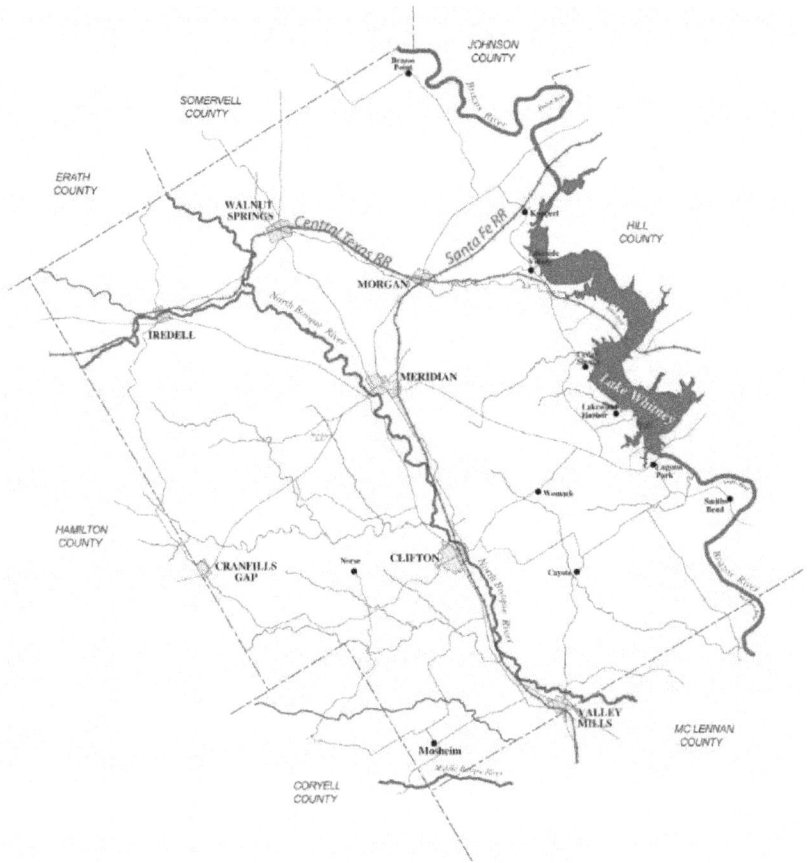

Bosque County Railroad Map
Property of The Bosque County Collection

ABOUT THE AUTHOR

T. L. Harrison moved to Bosque County, Texas after becoming a Sheriff's Deputy there in 2012. She felt an instant connection to the area and an intense curiosity for its rich history. She began her research for what would become *A Bloody History of Bosque County, Texas* in 2013 in an effort to uncover details of stories she heard from local residents. This led to the discovery of multiple recorded murders throughout Bosque County since the beginning of its history. Realizing the need to have these stories told, Harrison reviewed historical records to rediscover facts and complete fragmented accounts.

Follow on Facebook
http://facebook.com/tlharrisonauthor
http://facebook.com/A-Bloody-History-of-Bosque-County-Texas

Contact
tlharrisonauthor@gmail.com

REFERENCES

1 Historical Timeline for Bosque County, Courtesy Bosque County Historical Commission

2 Bosque County History Book Committee. *Bosque County: Land and People (A History of Bosque County, Texas)*, Book, 1985; digital images, (http://texashistory.unt.edu/ark:/67531/metapth91038/: accessed August 21, 2014), University of North Texas Libraries, The Portal to Texas History, http://texashistory.unt.edu; crediting Denton Public Library, Denton, Texas.

3 Bosque County History Book Committee. *Bosque County: Land and People (A History of Bosque County, Texas)*, Book, 1985; digital images, (http://texashistory.unt.edu/ark:/67531/metapth91038/: accessed August 21, 2014), University of North Texas Libraries, The Portal to Texas History, http://texashistory.unt.edu; crediting Denton Public Library, Denton, Texas.

4 Aragorn Storm Miller, "HELTON, JOSEPH KNOWLES," *Handbook of Texas Online* (http://www.tshaonline.org/handbook/online/articles/fhe91), accessed August 21, 2014. Uploaded on June 15, 2010. Published by the Texas State Historical Association.

5 1850 Federal Census, Courtesy of the Bosque County Historical Commission

6 Bosque County Deed Records, Courtesy of Bosque County Historical Society

7 Cureton, Early History of Bosque County, Courtesy of Bosque County

Historical Society

8 Presley Promissory Note, Courtesy of Bosque County Historical
   Society

9 Attachment for Bryant, Courtesy of Bosque County Historical Society

10 Attachment for Bryant, Courtesy of Bosque County Historical
    Society

11 Bryant Warrant, Courtesy of Bosque County Historical Society

12 *Galveston Weekly News (Galveston, Tex.)*, Vol. 12, No. 47, Ed. 1,
    Tuesday, January 29, 1856. Galveston, Texas. The Portal to Texas
    History. Http://texashistory.unt.edu/ark:/67531/metaphth79845/.
    Accessed August 21. 2014

13 Warrant for Abraham Kell, Courtesy of Bosque County Historical
    Society

14 Tidwell, Donovan Duncan. "Sunday Tragedy at the Bosque
    Church." *Iredell Times*, February 13, 1976.

15 Abstract District Court Minutes Smith County, Texas. Compiled by
    The East Texas Genealogical Society.

16 Tidwell, Donovan Duncan. "Sunday Tragedy at the Bosque
    Church." *Iredell Times*, February 13, 1976.

17 Tidwell, Donovan Duncan. "The Iredell Hanging." *Iredell Times*,
    March 5, 1976.

18 Tidwell, Donovan Duncan. "The Iredell Hanging." *Iredell Times*, March 5, 1976.

19 *Daily Democratic Statesman*, July 1, 1875.

20 *Dallas Weekly Herald*, August 14, 1875.

21 W.A.F. "Matters At Meridian." *The Galveston Daily News*, August 29, 1878.

22 "Bloody Murder In Bosque." *Lampasas Daily Times*, June 1, 1878.

23 "Murder of Storekeeper Vaughn In 1878 Remains Unsolved." *Meridian Tribune*, July 8, 1949.

24 Cranfill, James Britton. "The Vaughan Murder and Its Consequences." In *Dr. J.B. Cranfill's Chronicle*, 221. New York: Fleming H. Revell Company, 1916.

25 Cranfill, James Britton. "The Vaughan Murder and Its Consequences." In *Dr. J.B. Cranfill's Chronicle*, 221. New York: Fleming H. Revell Company, 1916.

26 Bosque County Historical Records, November Sheriff's and Collections

27 *Lampasas Daily Times*, June 5, 1878.

28 *Lampasas Daily Times*, June 15, 1878.

29 Cranfill, James Britton. "The Vaughan Murder and Its Consequences." In *Dr. J.B. Cranfill's Chronicle*, 222. New York:

Fleming H. Revell Company, 1916.

30 Cranfill, James Britton. "The Vaughan Murder and Its
Consequences." In *Dr. J.B. Cranfill's Chronicle*, 222. New York:
Fleming H. Revell Company, 1916.

31 Cranfill, James Britton. "The Vaughan Murder and Its
Consequences." In *Dr. J.B. Cranfill's Chronicle*, 222. New York:
Fleming H. Revell Company, 1916.

32 Cranfill, James Britton. "The Vaughan Murder and Its
Consequences." In *Dr. J.B. Cranfill's Chronicle*, 222. New York:
Fleming H. Revell Company, 1916.

33 *Lampasas Daily Times*, June 18, 1878.

34 Cranfill, James Britton. "The Vaughan Murder and Its
Consequences." In *Dr. J.B. Cranfill's Chronicle*, 223. New York:
Fleming H. Revell Company, 1916.

35 *Lampasas Daily Times*, June 18, 1878.

36 *Lampasas Daily Times*, June 23, 1878.

37 Cranfill, James Britton. "The Vaughan Murder and Its
Consequences." In *Dr. J.B. Cranfill's Chronicle*, 227-228. New York:
Fleming H. Revell Company, 1916.

38 "Another Arrest for the Vaughn Murder." *The Galveston Daily News*,
August 29, 1878, Matters At Meridian sec.

39 *Lampasas Daily Times*, July 6, 1878.

40 *Lampasas Daily Times*, August 22, 1878.

41 Downs, J. W., editor. *The Waco Daily Examiner. (Waco, Tex.), Vol. 7, No. 148, Ed. 1, Tuesday, December 3, 1878*, Newspaper, December 3, 1878

42 Field, William T. Jr., "The Texas State Police, 1870-1873), *Texas Military History 5* (Fall 1965).

43 Weiser, Kathy. "The Lawless Horrell Boys of Lampasas." Legends of America. March 1, 2014. Accessed August 31, 2014. http://www.legendsofamerica.com/tx-horrellbrothers.html.

44 "Custody of the Horrells (Special Correspondence of the News)." *The Galveston Daily News*, October 13, 1878, Letter From Meridian sec.

45 Sonnischsen, C.L. *I'll Die Before I'll Run: The Story of the Great Feuds of Texas*. New York: Harper & Brothers Publishers. 116-117.

46 Bosque County History Book Committee. Bosque County: Land and People (A History of Bosque County, Texas), Book, 1985; digital images, (http://texashistory.unt.edu/ark:/67531/metapth91038/ : accessed September 03, 2014), University of North Texas Libraries, The Portal to Texas History, http://texashistory.unt.edu; crediting Denton Public Library, Denton, Texas

47 Bosque County History Book Committee. Bosque County: Land and People (A History of Bosque County, Texas), Book, 1985; digital images, (http://texashistory.unt.edu/ark:/67531/metapth91038/ : accessed September 03, 2014), University of North Texas Libraries, The Portal to Texas History, http://texashistory.unt.edu; crediting

Denton Public Library, Denton, Texas

48 Bosque County History Book Committee. Bosque County: Land and People (A History of Bosque County, Texas), Book, 1985; digital images, (http://texashistory.unt.edu/ark:/67531/metapth91038/ : accessed September 03, 2014), University of North Texas Libraries, The Portal to Texas History, http://texashistory.unt.edu; crediting Denton Public Library, Denton, Texas

49 Bosque County Register of Elected and County Officials 1898-1900, Election Returns: November 8, 1898

50 "Deputy Sheriff Bob Conley Shot and Killed." *Meridian Tribune*, July 14, 1899.

51 "Deputy Sheriff Bob Conley Shot and Killed." *Meridian Tribune*, July 14, 1899.

52 "Historical Codes." Texas State Law Library. Accessed September 3, 2014.

53 "Historical Codes." Texas State Law Library. Accessed September 3, 2014.

54 Inmate Record of Ed Burrow, Texas Prison Museum Inmate Records, Research by Elizabeth Neucere

55 Bosque County History Book Committee. Bosque County: Land and People (A History of Bosque County, Texas), Book, 1985; digital images, (http://texashistory.unt.edu/ark:/67531/metapth91038/ : accessed October 02, 2014), University of North Texas Libraries, The

Portal to Texas History, http://texashistory.unt.edu; crediting Denton Public Library, Denton, Texas.

56 Bosque County History Book Committee. Bosque County: Land and People (A History of Bosque County, Texas), Book, 1985; digital images, (http://texashistory.unt.edu/ark:/67531/metapth91038/ : accessed October 02, 2014), University of North Texas Libraries, The Portal to Texas History, http://texashistory.unt.edu; crediting Denton Public Library, Denton, Texas.

57 Bosque County History Book Committee. Bosque County: Land and People (A History of Bosque County, Texas), Book, 1985; digital images, (http://texashistory.unt.edu/ark:/67531/metapth91038/ : accessed October 02, 2014), University of North Texas Libraries, The Portal to Texas History, http://texashistory.unt.edu; crediting Denton Public Library, Denton, Texas.

58 Letter from Mae (Jackson) Stowe, *The Walnut Springs Hustler*

59 *The Meridian Tribune.* (Meridian, Tex.), Vol. 7, No. 46, Ed. 1 Friday, April 25, 1902

60 *The Meridian Tribune.* (Meridian, Tex.), Vol. 7, No. 46, Ed. 1 Friday, April 25, 1902

61 *The Meridian Tribune.* (Meridian, Tex.), Vol. 7, No. 46, Ed. 1 Friday, April 25, 1902

62 Bosque County History Book Committee. Bosque County: Land and People (A History of Bosque County, Texas), Book, 1985; digital images, (http://texashistory.unt.edu/ark:/67531/metapth91038/ :

accessed October 03, 2014), University of North Texas Libraries, The Portal to Texas History, http://texashistory.unt.edu; crediting Denton Public Library, Denton, Texas.

63 Written recollections from an unidentified family member, owned by Sandford Ethridge (1993) courtesy of Bosque County Historical Society

64 "Mrs. Ethridge Made Confession", *The Meridian Tribune*, October 17, 1913

65 Written recollections from an unidentified family member, owned by Sandford Ethridge (1993) courtesy of Bosque County Historical Society

66 "Two Children Died Suddenly", *The Meridian Tribune*, October 10, 1913

67 "Mrs. Ethridge Made Confession", *The Meridian Tribune*, October 17, 1913

68 "Mrs. Ethridge Made Confession", *The Meridian Tribune*, October 17, 1913

69 "Two Children Died Suddenly", *The Meridian Tribune*, October 10, 1913

70 "Mrs. Ethridge Made Confession", *The Meridian Tribune*, October 17, 1913

71 "Two Children Died Suddenly", *The Meridian Tribune*, October 10,

1913

72 "Two Children Died Suddenly", *The Meridian Tribune*, October 10, 1913

73 "Bosque County Case is Serious", *Waco Times-Herald*, October 11, 1913

74 "Bosque County Case is Serious", *Waco Times-Herald*, October 11, 1913

75 "Mrs. Ethridge Made Confession", *The Meridian Tribune*, October 17, 1913

76 "Imprisonment for Life is Punishment Jury Gave Mrs. Ethridge", *Waco Times-Herald*, December 23, 1913

77 Inmate Record of Ellen Ethridge, Texas Prison Museum Inmate Records, Research by Elizabeth Neucere

78 Written recollections from an unidentified family member, owned by Sandford Ethridge (1993) courtesy of Bosque County Historical Society

79 Bosque County History Book Committee. *Bosque County: Land and People (A History of Bosque County, Texas)*, Book, 1985; digital images, (http://texashistory.unt.edu/ark:/67531/metapth91038/ : accessed September 18, 2014), University of North Texas Libraries, The Portal to Texas History, http://texashistory.unt.edu; crediting Denton Public Library, Denton, Texas.

80 *Houston Daily Post*, November 24, 1899.

81 *The Meridian Tribune*, January 5, 1900.

82 *The Meridian Tribune*, January 26, 1900.

83 *The Meridian Tribune*, February 16, 1900.

84 "W.T. Hix Killed at Smith's Bend." *The Meridian Tribune*, June 12, 1914.

85 "Another Version of the W. T. Hix Killing." *The Meridian Tribune*, June 19, 1914.

86 Natalie Ornish, "DE CORDOVA, JACOB RAPHAEL," *Handbook of Texas Online* (http://www.tshaonline.org/handbookonline/articles/fde03), accessed September 21, 2014. Uploaded on June 12, 2010. Published by the Texas State Historical Association.

87 Karen Yancy, "KIMBALL, TX" *Handbook of Texas Online* (http://www.tshaonlineorg/handbok/online/articles/hrk11), accessed September 01, 2014. Uploaded on June, 15, 2010. Published by the Texas State Historical Association.

88 Donald E Worcester, "CHISHOLM TRAIL" *Handbook of Texas Online* (http://www.tshaonlineorg/handbok/online/articles/hrk11), accessed September 01, 2014. Uploaded on June, 12, 2010. Published by the Texas State Historical Association.

89 Karen Yancy, "KIMBALL, TX" *Handbook of Texas Online*

(http://www.tshaonlineorg/handbok/online/articles/hrk11), accessed September 01, 2014. Uploaded on June, 15, 2010. Published by the Texas State Historical Association.

90 "Mrs. Nora Bosche Killed Step Daughter Tuesday." *The Meridian Tribune*, October 26, 1923.

91 "Mrs. Nora Bosche Killed Step Daughter Tuesday." *The Meridian Tribune*, October 26, 1923.

92 "Mrs. Nora Bosche Killed Step Daughter Tuesday." *The Meridian Tribune*, October 26, 1923.

93 "Man to Learn in Ninety Days of the Death of Wife." *The Clifton Record*, November 2, 1923.

94 "Mrs. Bosche Indicted on Charge of Murder." *The Meridian Tribune*, December 7, 1923.

95 "Mrs. Bosche Murder Case Was Continued." *The Meridian Tribune*, December 21, 1923.

96 "Mrs. Nora Bosche Released on Bond." *The Meridian Tribune*, January 18, 1924.

97 "Mrs. Bosche Brought Here From Oklahoma." *The Meridian Tribune*, April 4, 1924.

98 Jordan, William T. "Memories of Kopperl Killing Stay with Former County Attorney." *The Bosque Globe*, July 7, 1983, Anniversary Is Nearing sec.

99 "Woman Found Guilty on Murder Charge and Given 20 Years in the Pen." *The Meridian Tribune*, April 18, 1924.

100 Inmate Record of Nora Bosche, Texas Prison Museum Inmate Records, Research by Elizabeth Neucere

101 "Pardon Sought For Mrs. Boesche" *The Meridian Tribune*, January 14, 1927

102 Inmate Record of Nora Bosche, Texas Prison Museum Inmate Records, Research by Elizabeth Neucere

103 "Mrs. Bosche Awaits Pardon to Wed Lover." *The Meridian Tribune*, July 5, 1929.

104 "Mrs. Boesche Marries Ex-Convict in Prison." *The Meridian Tribune*, July 29, 1929.

105 "Mrs. Boesche Marries Ex-Convict in Prison." *The Meridian Tribune*, July 29, 1929.

106 Kristi Strickland, "BOSQUE COUNTY," *Handbook of Texas Online* (http://www.tshaonline.org/handbook/online/articles/hcb10), accessed September 25, 2014. Uploaded on June 12, 2010. Modified on March 26, 2014. Published by the Texas State Historical Association.

107 *The Meridian Tribune* (Meridian, Tex.), Vol. 42, No. 27, Ed. 1 Friday, November 29, 1935, Newspaper, November 29, 1935; digital images, (http://texashistory.unt.edu/ark:/67531/metapth341965/:

accessed September 25, 2014), University of North Texas Libraries, The Portal to Texas History, http://texashistory.unt.edu; crediting Meridian Public Library, Meridian, Texas.

108   Benson, Sheriff Pearl. "The Black Things." *Inside Detective*, November 1, 1937, 34-52.

109   Benson, Sheriff Pearl. "The Black Things." *Inside Detective*, November 1, 1937, 34-52.

110   "Couple Held Without Bail on Poison Murder Charge." *The Meridian Tribune*, May 1, 1936.

111   "Couple Held Without Bail on Poison Murder Charge." *The Meridian Tribune*, May 1, 1936.

112   "Heavy Docket Awaits Court." *The Meridian Tribune*, September 18, 1936.

113   "Poison Murder Trail Set for Next Wednesday; 7 Indicted." *The Meridian Tribune*, September 25, 1936.

114   "Mrs. Clomer Jermstad given 45 Years in Poison Murder." *The Meridian Tribune*, October 2, 1936.

115   "George Pace Gets 75-Year Term in Jermstad Poisoning." *The Meridian Tribune*, October 9, 1936.

116   Inmate Record of Clomer Jermstad, Texas Prison Museum Inmate Records, Research by Elizabeth Neucere

117 Inmate Record of George Pace, Texas Prison Museum Inmate Records, Research by Elizabeth Neucere

118 "Well Known Bosque Man Shot Dead" *The Meridian Tribune,* October 24, 1941.

119 1940 Federal Census, http://interactive.ancestry.com/2442/m-t0627-03988-00374/160204396?backurl=&ssrc=&backlabel=ReturnRecord, accessed 2 October 2014.

120 "Well Known Bosque Man Shot Dead" *The Meridian Tribune,* October 24, 1941.

121 "Jury Indicts Daughter in Death Case" *The Meridian Tribune,* March 20, 1942.

122 "Venire Is Called For Death Trial" *The Meridian Tribune,* April 3, 1942.

123 "Hornbuckle Death Case on Trial" *The Meridian Tribune,* April 10, 1942.

124 "Suspended Term Given Defendant" *The Meridian Tribune,* April 17, 1942.

125 "Son Charged with Death of His Father" *The Meridian Tribune,* October 9, 1942.

126 "Son Charged with Death of His Father" *The Meridian Tribune,* October 9, 1942.

127 "Lunacy Charge Against Howard P. Hornbuckle in County Court Dismissed" *The Meridian Tribune*, October 23, 1942.

128 "Howard Hornbuckle Insane, is Verdict of Trial Jury Here" *The Meridian Tribune*, December 18, 1942.

www.ingramcontent.com/pod-product-compliance
Lightning Source LLC
LaVergne TN
LVHW041155080426
835511LV00006B/618